Pewter flagon with the intials PRE
found in early 17th-century well
(Structure 170)

The Archaearium

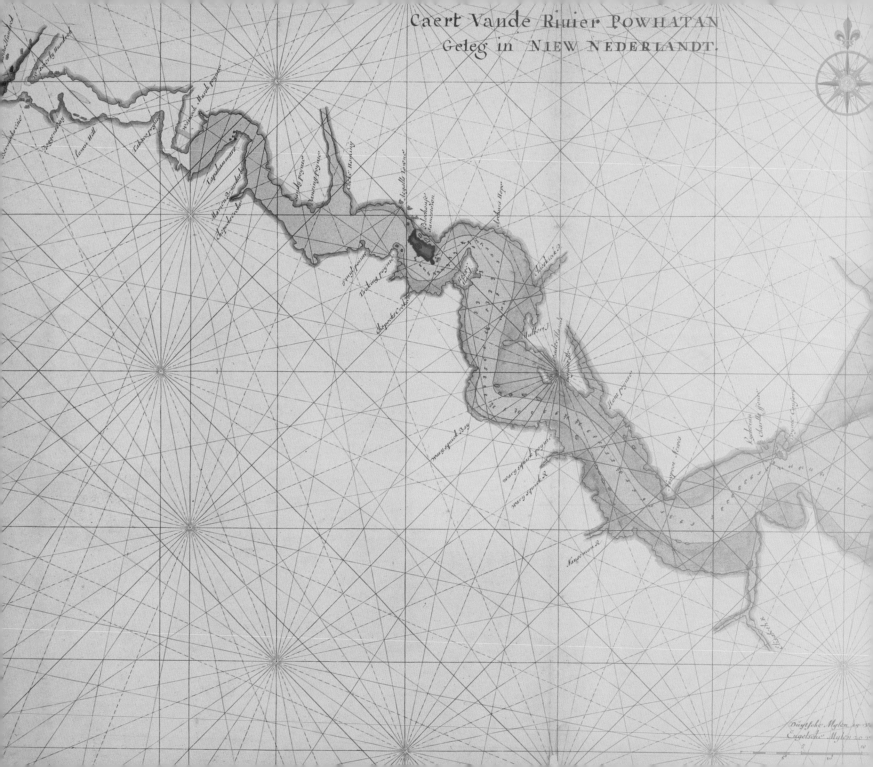

Caert Vande Rivier POWHATAN
Geleg in NIEW NEDERLANDT.

The Archaearium

Rediscovering Jamestown 1607–1699
Jamestown, Virginia

Beverly A. Straube

Curator's Note

Selection of the artifacts for this exhibition was in some ways very easy and, in others, extremely difficult. It was easy in that there were plenty of objects from which to choose. The *Jamestown Rediscovery* archaeological project has excavated nearly one million artifacts since its inception in 1994. But that also made my job very hard. There were too many choices! Never before has there been such a rich collection of material culture excavated from America's soils that is contextually related to the nation's English origins. These are the objects that were used, broken, discarded, and lost by the men, women, and children making up the fabric of England's first colony. Also represented are thousands of artifacts made by the Virginia Indians, visibly demonstrating how interwoven the two cultures became at early Jamestown.

In planning the exhibition with the designers, Haley Sharpe Design, it soon became apparent to us all that the material required a unique approach. These are the actual things from the real place and that contextual strength is important. So, rather than starting with a list of themes and selecting the artifacts from the collection that would best illustrate them, it was decided that the artifacts should lead the way. These wonderful objects have many stories to tell and the exhibition was designed around those stories. As a result, the artifacts are the stars as they reveal information about life and death in the fort, a site that is constantly in view through the large glass panes of the Archaearium.

To reinforce the direct relationship of the objects displayed in the Archaearium to James Fort, the museum has virtual viewers that visitors can use to scan the site. With the press of a button, the 17th-century fort appears, and the viewer zooms into a particular area with an interpretation of the archaeological findings.

Period quotes from the people who lived at James Fort supplement the artifacts throughout the museum, as do European paintings that illustrate various aspects of 17th-century life. Many of the artifacts are displayed in the context in which they were found, whether a well, a soldier's pit house, or the bulwark trench of the fort. In so doing, it is hoped that the public might share in those moments of discovery that the archaeologists experienced in the field. Visitors can see what the archaeologists saw and participate in the interpretive process as the findings are explained.

Many people have contributed to the success of the Archaearium, which would have never been realized without the sustained support of Elizabeth Kostelny, Executive Director of APVA Preservation Virginia, and the APVA's board of trustees. Bill Kelso, Director of Archaeology for *Jamestown Rediscovery*, enthusiastically contributed direction and assistance to the Archaearium's vision. Bill Haley and his very talented design team at Haley Sharpe Design fleshed out that vision with panache, and Carlton Abbott and his architectural firm Carlton Abbott and Partners provided the dramatic and unusual structure that is the Archaearium. Michael Lavin and Dan Gamble worked diligently to ensure that all the artifacts were conserved and stable. Mr. Lavin also advised the design team during installation of the artifacts. Caroline Taylor provided invaluable curatorial support in numbering, mending and packing up the objects for display. Tonia Deetz Rock and Ann Berry spent countless hours writing and editing text. Jamie May adeptly managed the graphics and Bonnie Lent patiently secured the necessary permissions. Dave Givens supplied unequalled technical support, especially with the development of the virtual viewers. With the help of these individuals, and many others, the Archaearium is a worthy gift to the people of America for the 400th anniversary of Jamestown's founding.

Beverly A. Straube FSA
Senior Curator, *Jamestown Rediscovery*
APVA Preservation Virginia

Designer's Note

The "power of place" is the essence of a visit to Historic Jamestowne. And the center point of that power is the site of the James Fort. There is an ethereal, almost magical feeling of standing at the very spot where modern America began. It is a feeling amplified by the exceptional archaeological remains and artifacts that have been found there. This tangible "stuff" of history makes the intangible sense of past people and events intensely close.

In the creation of exhibits for the Archaearium, this powerful feeling of place was always going to provide the most meaningful foundation. As interpretive designers, Haley Sharpe Design worked closely with the APVA Preservation Virginia team, and architects Carlton Abbott & Partners to enable visitors to get as close as possible to both archaeological structures and artifacts.

We wanted to ensure that these extraordinary objects "shone out" as the precious evidence that they are. We paid particular attention to the creation of mood and atmosphere. Dynamic lighting throws emphasis on significant objects, casts the shadows of artifacts across the floor, or supports feelings of wonder or reverence.

Graphics are bold, the many 17th-century painting images being integrated into a color palette of warm, earthy tones. We strove for an overall effect which would reflect the human drama represented by the artifacts. These displays are not in the end about time stood still, but about living communities caught up in an extraordinarily dynamic period in history.

The zones of the exhibition are based around specific archaeological contexts – sites of particular buildings, burials, pits and wells. Artifacts found together in one such context are displayed together, to help explain the archaeological process. By giving each such zone a distinct character, and linking it to wider themes, the stories of people can be naturally woven in.

The positioning of the Archaearium was also fundamental. It allows visitors to look out directly at the Fort site, to see from where the displayed artifacts have come. To further support this, we developed a new exhibit technology to allow visitors to interactively explore their view across to the Fort, through "virtual" reconstructions of the historic landscape. This immediacy of connection is unique, encouraging visitors to create imaginative linkages in their own minds between a 'triangle' of elements – the Fort, its artifacts, and the people who trod the site hundreds of years ago.

Throughout the project, the compelling sensation of being so close to past events and lives that were to change the world was always an inspiration to us. We hope it continues to be so for the Archaearium's visitors long into the future.

Bill Haley
Director, Haley Sharpe Design

Architect's Note

The site selected for the Archaearium is atop the ruins of the third and fourth Statehouse, Virginia's capitol from 1665-1699, and other known archaeological resources dating to the early seventeenth century. Dramatic views west to the James River and east to the historic James Fort archaeological site are compelling elements that informed the building design in combination with the subsurface resources.

The building is situated in a "clean zone"; meaning archaeological investigations were conducted but the resources were not necessarily removed from the site. A matrix of known resources and historic foundations informed a pile foundation that literally "threads the needle" to gain adequate bearing in the surrounding soils. Helical pulldown micropiles were used to provide maximum structural capacity. Additionally, the micropile installation technique enabled the remaining site and archaeology to be undisturbed by traffic or soil disturbance. This foundation technology with structural cantilevers allowed the building program of 8000 square feet to be achieved on the approximately 5000 square foot "clean" site.

The building's modern idiom arose from exhibit imperatives including views of James Fort and the associated "virtual viewer" exhibit technology, which reconstructs the historic James Fort with layers of information on the modern landscape through visitor-manipulated viewfinders. Also important were architectural decisions that the new structure defers to the formal language of the early 20th-century Yeardley and Dale houses, which share frontage with it on the historic Yeardley green. The building is of glass and copper, the latter cladding chosen as a sustainable alternative that is applied using traditional detail and gains richness appropriate to the historic site in its patina and deference to the landscape. Copper was also chosen in homage to its historical significance. It was vital to the early Jamestown colonists as an item of trade for food with the Virginia Indians.

Visually, the building bears lightly on the land because the structural system requires no perimeter-bearing wall. This "hovering" effect is enhanced by landscape strategies. The "prow" of the building, which reaches toward the James River, is deliberately placed to create an exciting raised vantage point from the museum to view the river, which was an important mode of transportation throughout the colonial period.

Many "green building" technologies were applied in the building design, including geothermal heating and cooling, reflective TPO roof technology, low water consumption, a high-performance building envelope, and the interior use of day lighting.

Finally, in respect to the historic resources, the building features "floor portals," where glimpses of the brick footings of the Statehouse can be seen through structural floor glazing within the exhibit. Contrasting floor finishes trace the foundations throughout the exhibit to remind the visitors of the historic building that lies beneath.

Carlton S. Abbott, FAIA
David M. Stemann, AIA
Carlton Abbott & Partners

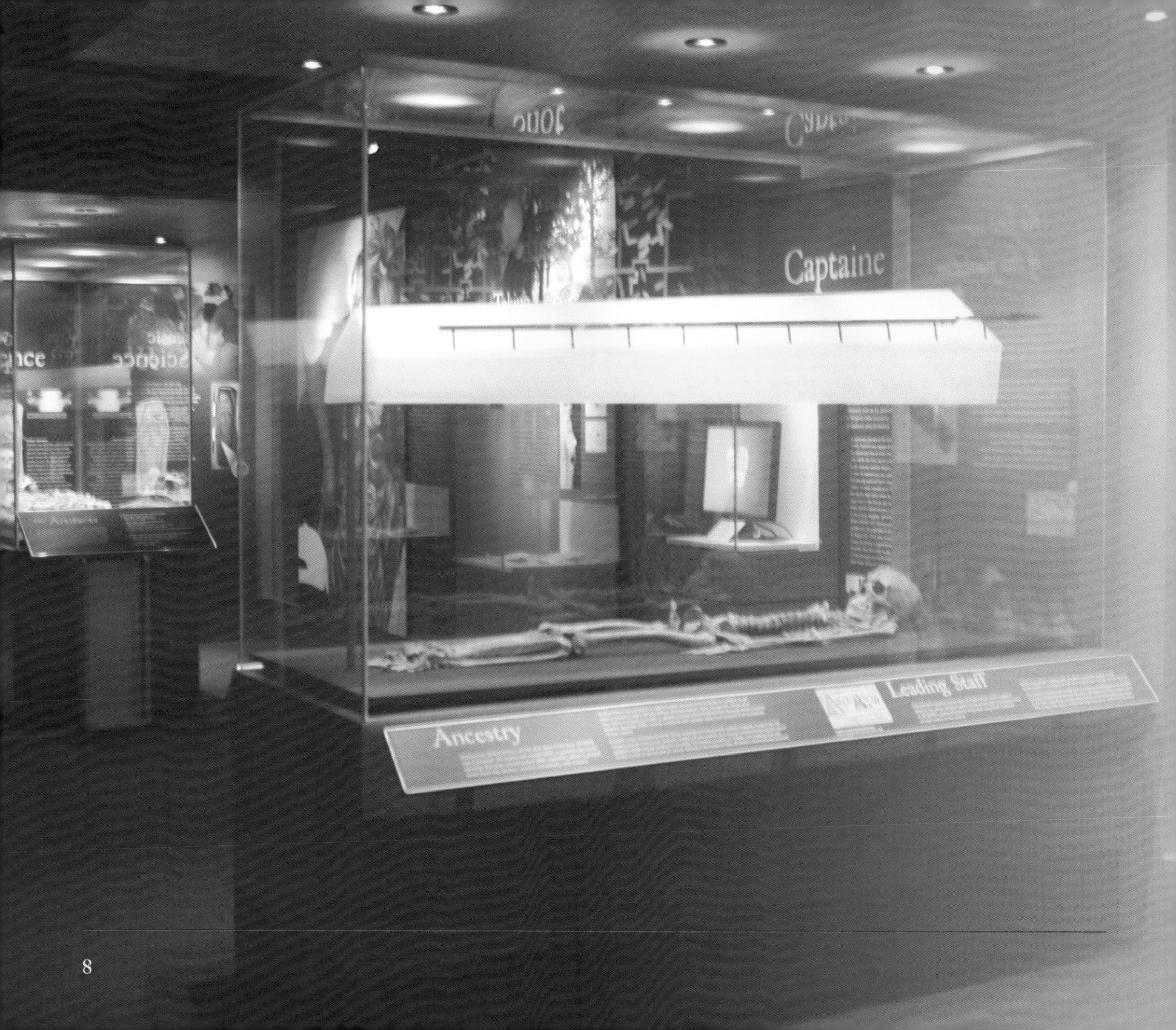
Captaine
Ancestry
Leading Staff

Table of Contents

The Archaearium

The Archaearium exhibition tells the story of the founding years of Jamestown as seen through the eyes of the people who lived here and the artifacts they left behind.

Archaearium (pronounced / är´-k ē-er´-ē-əm / n.) is a new word meaning "a place of beginnings" that was created to describe a unique place. The Archaearium is the museum for the archaeological findings of the *Jamestown Rediscovery* project's excavations at Historic Jamestowne. These excavations, on the 22 acres of Jamestown Island belonging to APVA Preservation Virginia, began in 1994 and have succeeded in finding James Fort, the most important archaeological site relating to America's colonial past. Established by the English in 1607, James Fort was the first location of the Virginia colony that managed to survive and grow into the nation we know today as the United States of America.

For the past 200 years, the site of America's beginnings was thought lost forever, eroded away by the James River. Now, archaeologists are uncovering remnants of the fort as well as foundations of Jamestown's buildings, which date from the beginning to the end of the 17th century. From these foundations, as well as from cellars, trash pits and wells have been found hundreds of thousands of artifacts illustrating life at Jamestown from its beginnings in 1607 to 1699, when the colony's capital moved to Williamsburg.

Even though most of Jamestown's people could not record their own experiences, and the details of their lives are unknown to history, they left evidence of their existence for archaeologists to interpret. In the colonists' trash, archaeologists are finding many clues they can piece together. These include remnants of weaponry and tools, remains of meals, fragments of pottery and glassware, pieces of jewelry and clothing and bits of musical instruments and games. For centuries these objects remained below the earth's surface just out of reach. Now they can, at last, begin to tell the story of Jamestown.

The Virginia Company

King James I granted a charter in April 1605 to the Virginia Company for exploration, trade, and settlement in Virginia, an area of North America that today stretches from Maine to North Carolina. Headquartered in London, the Virginia Company consisted of gentlemen, nobles, and merchants who hoped the colony would provide financial gain for them as well as for England.

The Virginia Company planned, funded, and recruited for the colonizing effort. Substantial information on North America had been amassed in planning the venture, yet much remained unknown. Knowledge of Canada, Florida, New England, and the Carolinas was available from earlier French, Spanish and English explorations. But little was known about the target area for settlement — the Chesapeake Bay. The initial settlement was, by necessity, exploratory.

> *"The seventh day, we arrived at Mona: where wee watered, which we stood in great need of, seeing that our water did smell so vildly that none of our men was able to indure it."*
>
> *George Percy, 1607*

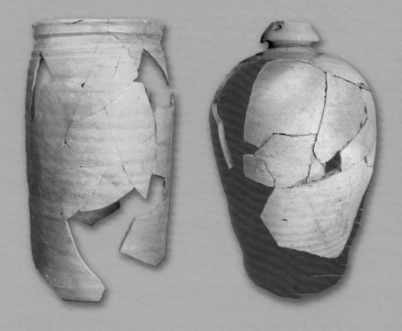

Crossing the Atlantic

Following a route to the Americas similar to that of Columbus, the first colonists arrived in Virginia after a voyage lasting five months.

Leaving London in December 1606, the colonists first sailed south to the Canary Islands off the coast of Africa. Pushed by the trade winds, they crossed the Atlantic to the West Indies. There they stopped to take on fresh water and supplies. A northerly sail along the east coast of America brought them to the Chesapeake Bay in 16 days. The men finally arrived at Jamestown on May 13, 1607.

Even though the southern course through the Canaries took twice as long as the northern route, it was easier to navigate because of fewer storms. It also enabled sea-weary sailors to island-hop along the way, stopping to fill the ships' casks with fresh water and to trade with natives for food.

"...be not hasty in Landing..."
The Virginia Company, 1606

Site Selection

Although they had no detailed knowledge of the Chesapeake Bay area, the Virginia Company sent their colonists off with general guidelines to settle in a profitable and safe locale. The company warned the colonists to locate a navigable river but "be not hasty in landing" until they found the best site.

The expedition first landed on April 26, 1607, at Cape Henry, near where the Chesapeake Bay enters the Atlantic Ocean. Following the Virginia Company suggestion to settle "a hundred miles from the Rivers mouth," the ships then entered the bay and sailed about 70 miles up the James River before turning back. They were unable to find a suitable location that far upriver that would both insure security from the much-feared Spanish and that would not interfere with any Indian settlement. The Virginia Company advised the colonists "to have great care not to offend the naturals" as they hoped to sustain the colony by trading with the Virginia Indians for food.

Jamestown Island, the site preferred by the colonist with the highest seniority, Edward Maria Wingfield, was finally selected. Despite its marshes and lack of freshwater springs, it was the best strategic location for the settlement because:

- As an island that became an isthmus at low tide, it fit the Company suggestion for a defensible settlement on "Some Island that is Strong by Nature." A blockhouse defended the narrow land bridge.

- Even though the fort stood only 36 miles from the mouth of the river, not the 100 miles suggested by the Virginia Company, because of tides, winds, and bends in the river it took almost a day to sail the distance. This provided time for sentinels to give advance warning of any approaching enemy ships.

- Hog Island screened the island from view of ships sailing upriver. A blockhouse on Hog Island provided clear line-of-sight for over 15 miles down the river and served as a lookout for approaching ships.

- Navigation in the James River is limited to a narrow channel that meanders from one side to the other. The channel runs closest to the shore at the western end of the island, convenient to the fort. This was a deciding factor according to colonist George Percy who said "our ships do lie so near the shore that they are moored to the trees." The channel also forced any approaching enemy ships to sail within range of the fort's artillery.

"Virginia, Earth's onely Paradise."

Michael Drayton, 1608

"{The Powhatan} are a very witty and ingenious people apt both to understand and speak our language . . ."

Gabriel Archer, 1607

The Landing

On May 13, 1607, over 100 men and boys marched ashore on Jamestown Island and changed the course of modern history. Virginia looked like Paradise to the colonists. The quantity and variety of plants and animals prompted one colonist to remark "God hath filled the elements of the earth, aire, and waters with his creatures, good for our food and nourishment." Described as "excellent and verie Rich in gold and Copper," Virginia also had other commodities like wood, sassafras, and pearls that the Virginia Company hoped to market. In addition, most of the Virginia Indians welcomed rather than threatened the settling effort. The English had landed in the territory of the Paspahegh Indians and, according to colonist George Percy, within four days the werwowance, or chief, arrived and "made signes that he would give us as much land as we would desire to take."

Feeling no immediate threat from the Virginia Indians, the colonists initially had "no exercise of arms, or fortification but the boughs of trees cast together in the forme of a halfe moon." Within two weeks a force of over 200 Indians attacked, wounding ten colonists and killing two. "Hereupon," John Smith records, "the President [Wingfield] was contented the Fort should be pallisadoed."

"the thirteenth day, we came to our seating place in Paspihas Countrey . . ."

George Percy, 1607

"The have fortified themselves
and built a small towne which
they call James-towne . . ."

Dudley Carleton, 1607

> *"... the fort is called in honor of His Majesty's name, James Town."*
> William Strachey, 1610.

The Fort

By June 15th, Jamestown became a fortified outpost. Upright, split or unhewn oak and walnut fourteen-foot timbers formed the protective wall or palisade of the fort. This palisade, enclosing over an acre, framed the settlement in a large triangle. The wall along the river's edge was the longest at 140 yards, with the east and west sides measuring 100 yards each. Each corner had a bulwark for cannon and a system of outworks created with ditches. The cannon fired solid iron balls known as shot. Since the non-exploding shot would be of little help against Virginia Indian attacks, the cannon were placed to fire long and low over the river, thereby protecting the fort from approaching enemy ships.

As archaeologists began removing the centuries of dirt from the site in 1994, they quickly realized they were uncovering the remains of James Fort. Not only did the stains in the ground match the wooden defensive walls described by the colonists, but also the objects found indicated that James Fort had been found. There were many hundreds of artifacts dating to the late 16th and early 17th centuries and most were military.

> *"... three Bulwarkes at every corner like a half Moone, and four or five pieces of Artillerie mounted in them."*
> George Percy, 1607

" . . . well trained and expert souldiers"
Richard Potts and William Pettiplace, 1609

Military venture

Because Jamestown was both a business enterprise and a military venture, a significant percentage of the first colonists were "well trained and expert souldiers." The frontier colony needed military men to protect against the actuality of Indian assaults and the possibility of Spanish attack.

Arms and armor were essential to the colony and a wealth of military equipment was found in early fort contexts. These include private arms, which probably belonged to the gentlemen, and military issue weapons for the rank and file soldier. The new conditions of the frontier settlement meant outmoded and archaic weaponry was as useful as up-to-date equipment.

"... worthy and noble gentlemen ..."

William Strachey, 1610

Gentlemen Soldiers

About half of the colonists sent to Virginia in the first few years are identified as gentlemen, men often blamed by historians for not contributing to the sustainability of the colony. But gentlemen played essential roles in the military colony – protection and leadership.

At times the gentlemen probably were reluctant to help with chores requiring hard labor; after all, these were not jobs they had been sent to do. Gentlemen safeguarded the rest of the colonists as they worked to profit the investors. But according to colonist William Strachey, the laborers and craftsmen expected these "worthy and noble gentlemen [to] no less help them with their hand than defend them with the sword." The Virginia frontier challenged traditional roles and expectations.

In the early 17th century those of gentle birth found a military profession quite suitable. Gentlemen commanded troops and decided on tactics. Jamestown's gentlemen, experienced from the battlegrounds of Europe, came equipped to fight using up-to-date arms, armor, and methods of warfare.

Most of the gentlemen at Jamestown, including all the members of the governing council, had seen action in recent battles in the Netherlands, fighting on the side of Dutch Protestants against Spain. Some, like Edward Maria Wingfield, the first president of the council in Virginia, also participated in Irish campaigns. Many of these veterans brought their personal arms to Jamestown rather than rely on cheaper military-issue weapons provided by the company.

"... *a valiant Gentleman.*"

Gabriel Archer, 1607

Edward Maria Wingfield

Edward Maria Wingfield is representative of Jamestown's gentleman soldier. He came from a distinguished family with a long history of soldiering, and had served in both Ireland and the Low Countries. Those experiences turned him into an advocate for colonizing North America. He was among the leaders who solicited James I to charter the Virginia Company of London.

The company appointed him to the colony's resident council, which made him the sole company officer ever to go to America. His standing explains why his fellow councilors elected him as their first president once they arrived in Virginia and why they deferred to his decision to plant the settlement on Jamestown Island. Despite those promising beginnings, within months the difficulties of governing a colony wracked with dissension were overwhelming and he was displaced. He returned to England on the first opportunity in April 1608, in John Smith's words, "to seeke some better place of imploiment." The challenges presented in the new colony were equalizing forces in the transplanted English social structure.

The People of Jamestown

Who landed on Jamestown's shores after 1607? Mostly English, Jamestown's colonists had diverse social backgrounds, from wealthy aristocracy to poor unskilled laborers. Some intended to stay for good, some for just the short term, some had no option to leave. Most individuals came willingly, to join family members or in search of economic opportunity. Others, forced from their homeland, arrived against their will. Archaeology offers insight into the lives of rich and poor, known and unknown, willing and coerced.

Documents tell us generally about Jamestown's colonists. Skeletal remains literally bring us face to face with Jamestown's people, especially those poor and illiterate unable to write about their own experiences. Through the archaeological and forensic study of skeletal remains, we can determine many things about a person, including age, general health, and even physical appearance.

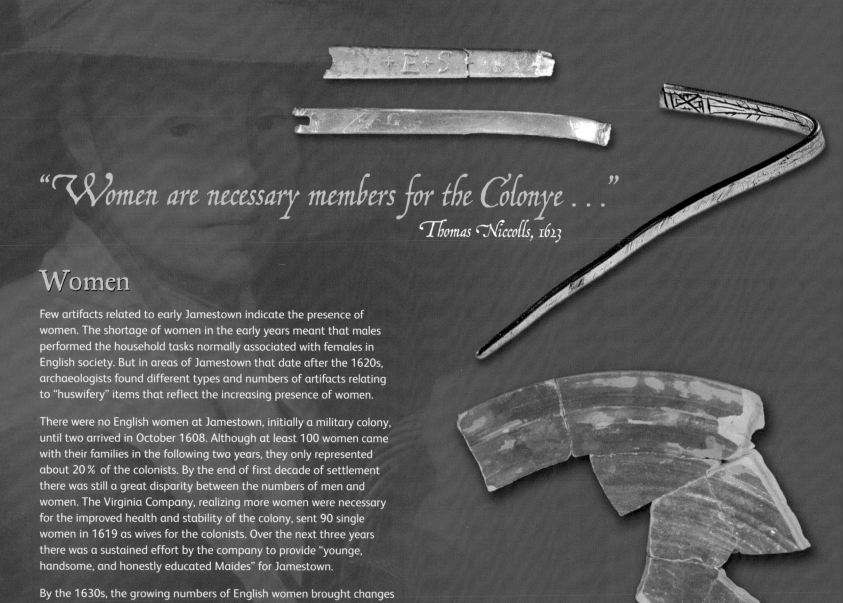

"Women are necessary members for the Colonye ..."

Thomas Niccolls, 1623

Women

Few artifacts related to early Jamestown indicate the presence of women. The shortage of women in the early years meant that males performed the household tasks normally associated with females in English society. But in areas of Jamestown that date after the 1620s, archaeologists found different types and numbers of artifacts relating to "huswifery" items that reflect the increasing presence of women.

There were no English women at Jamestown, initially a military colony, until two arrived in October 1608. Although at least 100 women came with their families in the following two years, they only represented about 20 % of the colonists. By the end of first decade of settlement there was still a great disparity between the numbers of men and women. The Virginia Company, realizing more women were necessary for the improved health and stability of the colony, sent 90 single women in 1619 as wives for the colonists. Over the next three years there was a sustained effort by the company to provide "younge, handsome, and honestly educated Maides" for Jamestown.

By the 1630s, the growing numbers of English women brought changes reflected in artifacts. For example, the increased number of milk pans used for collecting milk and processing it into cream and cheese indicates greater emphasis on dairying activities, a female task.

"'No mournful bell shall ring her burial . . ."
William Shakespeare

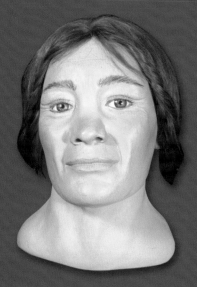

JR156C

The burial of a woman (identified by her archaeological field designation JR156C) was found within the walls of James Fort. We will probably never know her name, but we can learn a lot about her by studying her remains.

Forensic analysis shows that she:
- was European
- was 40 to 55 years old
- was 4' 8" tall
- died of unknown causes
- had only five teeth when she died and had lived without her missing teeth for a long time
- had a lifetime of strenuous work
- was probably buried in the 1620s

Even though she had to work hard during her lifetime, JR156C was apparently a woman of status in the colonial society. Her coffin and teeth indicate this. Pieces of the surviving coffin wood and nails in the grave shaft show that she was buried in a gable-lidded coffin, a type associated in the 17th century with higher status burials. Her lack of teeth, which today we might associate with poverty, could indicate that she was wealthy enough to afford expensive but tooth-damaging sugar.

". . . usual burying place by James City."
John Atkins, 1623

Burial Ground

Interpretation of the Jamestown population from skeletal remains requires study of more than just a few individual burials. So archaeologists recovered and analyzed a statistical sample of over 50 individuals from an unmarked burial ground located below the foundations of Jamestown's Statehouse.

In place by the 1660s, this complex of buildings suggests that by then the burial ground upon which they were built had long since gone out of use. This may be the graveyard referred to in 1623 as the "usual burying place by James City."

By studying these burials, archaeologists look for vital statistics about the early colonists including:

- the ratio of women to men
- ancestry
- social and economic status
- life expectancy
- percentages of settlers born in England versus Virginia
- general health
- common diseases
- causes of death
- burial customs

Beyond revealing data on the people of Jamestown, this information will be used to compare and contrast with other early English settlements in the Chesapeake region and around the world.

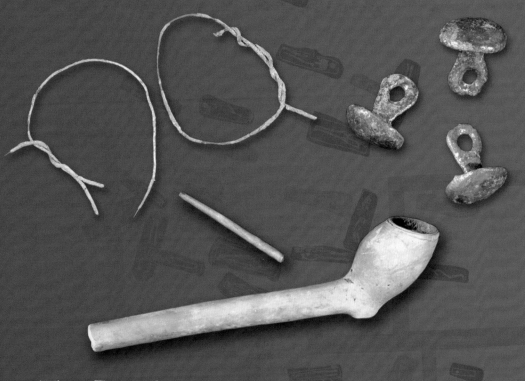

The Burials

The Statehouse Burial Project has added insightful knowledge of early 17th-century Jamestown. Archaeologists, historians, and forensic scientists will use this wealth of data for long-term scientific studies.

The burials reflect a cross-section of Jamestown's population. Most are adult males who died in their mid-20s. This information is revealing when compared to estimates of life expectancy in 17th-century London, the city from which most of them came. The average age of death for wealthy London males was 30–35 years, with more affluent individuals surviving into their 50s. The life expectancy for men from the poorer sections of the city was only 20–25, which is a bit lower than the ages of the Jamestown males. From this, it appears that wealthy males fared worse and poorer males fared better at Jamestown than they would have at home.

The females are a few years older than the males at death, perhaps reflecting the older population of women who emigrated to Jamestown. The rest of those studied include infants, younger teens, and middle-aged adults. Evidence of death or illness from disease, malnutrition, and even violence was found.

The study also revealed burial practices. Seven individuals were buried in coffins, indicating a higher social status. But most were just placed in the ground, many wrapped in cloth shrouds. A few were buried in their clothing, a very unusual practice at the time except when the individual died of a contagious disease. It appears that all of these early colonists lived difficult lives, and the few who had social advantages fared little better than others.

Captain Bartholomew Gosnold

While searching for the west wall of James Fort, archaeologists discovered an isolated grave. Two facts indicated that the burial, designated JR1046B, was an early one. It was parallel to the palisade, which meant the fort wall was standing when the grave was prepared. A trash pit had been dug over the burial in the 1630s, which indicated by then the gravesite was very old and long forgotten.

This was not a typical burial. Excavation revealed evidence of a well-built, gable-lidded coffin upon which someone had carefully placed a ceremonial staff. A captain carries this type of object as a sign of his rank. Were these the remains of Captain Bartholomew Gosnold, the man identified as "the first mover of this plantation" by John Smith?

History has overlooked Bartholomew Gosnold because he died three months after Jamestown was settled. His roles as a promoter of the Virginia Company and as an adventurer to Virginia were crucial to Jamestown and its history.

As a primary planner of the Jamestown colony, Gosnold was captain of the Godspeed and one of seven men selected for the first council in Virginia. By the time he reached Virginia in 1607, he was an experienced sea captain who had already explored North American waters. An early expedition in 1602 led him up the east coast, where he named Cape Cod for the fish he saw swimming there, and the island Martha's Vineyard for his young daughter.

Identified by a fellow colonist as a "worthy and religious gentleman," Gosnold died at the age of 36 at Jamestown on August 22, 1607, after a three-week illness. According to eyewitnesses, Gosnold "was honorably buried, having all the Ordnance in the Fort shot off, with many vollies of small shot."

" *...the first mover of this plantation..."*
John Smith, 1612

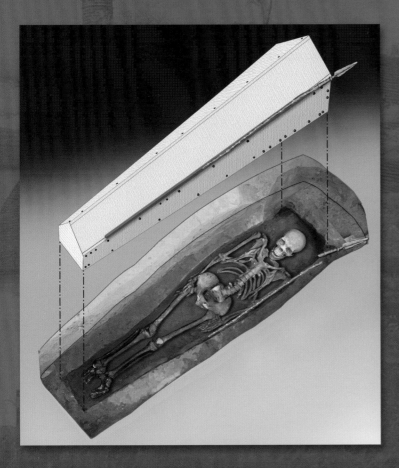

JR1046B

A chain of forensic evidence linked to the burial offers even more reason to believe that JR1046B is Bartholomew Gosnold. But how can skeletal remains hold clues to identity after 400 years in the ground? To forensic scientists, the bones can read almost like a biography. They can determine:

- **Sex** This skeleton was clearly a male, having a robust skull, with distinct angles on the jaw. Additionally, the pelvis is narrow and deep unlike a female's pelvis that is wide and shallow enough to accommodate childbirth.

- **Age** The presence of the wisdom teeth, or third molars, indicates that this individual was an adult. Well-preserved pelvic development establishes that his death occurred in his mid thirties. The ends of the thighbones were all completely attached or fused, again confirming that this is a fully developed adult.

- **Status** Despite healed injuries to JR1046B's ankle, wrist and back, his overall bone development reflects the healthy but not necessarily inactive life of a gentleman.

- **Ancestry** Distinctive characteristics of the skull determine that JR1046B was European. His bones still carry DNA, a possible key to his identity. But only mitochondrial DNA (mtDNA), which is passed down from the mother, survives reasonably well in bone. To determine if this individual is indeed Captain Bartholomew Gosnold, his mtDNA would need to match his direct female relatives. A search for the remains of Gosnold's sister, Elizabeth Gosnold Tilney who is buried in Shelly Church, Suffolk England, proved inconclusive. However, analysis of the remains of a woman uncovered during this search yielded a stable isotope reading for an early 17th-century resident of Suffolk. This reading was very similar to that of JR1046B adding to the evidence that it is Bartholomew Gosnold.

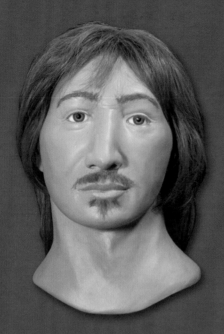

JR

The first burial unearthed in the fort was JR102C, who quickly became known as JR, for the "Jamestown Rediscovery" part of his field number. The skeleton is of a young European male and, unlike most excavated burials, his cause of death is visible.

JR was 5' 9", slightly taller than the average Englishman of the period. His bones show that he was a gentleman, and moderately fit but not accustomed to hard labor. His burial in a coffin also suggests JR was a person of higher status.

A lead bullet still lodged in the bone of JR's lower right leg indicates that he was wounded at the time of his death. Forensic examination of the wound determined that the bullet entered the right side of his leg just below the knee. An X-ray of the injury revealed several additional small pieces of lead embedded in the bone. The impact of the gunshot smashed the bone and probably severed an artery. JR's leg shows no sign of any surgery, infection, or healing suggesting that this traumatic injury led to his immediate death.

Taking a Shot

How was the young man known as JR shot? Controlled ballistic tests revealed clues to the cause of his fatal injury.

The "ball and shot" spread pattern imbedded in JR's leg bones was a key to determining what kind of weapon wounded him, and the distance between the gun and its victim. A number of test shots, using reproduction 17th-century guns fired at different distances, attempted to replicate the lead pattern in the wound.

A pistol produced the right shot pattern at a distance of eight feet and a caliver (small musket) the same pattern at 15 feet. This pattern not only identified possible weapon types, but also proved that JR did not accidentally shoot himself. These weapons and distances suggest that JR was probably shot accidentally while either hunting or engaged in military exercises. Or, he could well have been a casualty of infighting during Jamestown's more stressful times.

Forensic science can also help us know more about JR:

- **Carbon dating** A test called C-14 dating can tell approximately when someone died by measuring the carbon left in the bone. Humans take in carbon by eating plants and animals. When a person dies, the carbon disintegrates. The carbon dating for JR indicates that he could have died as early as 1607. Other evidence puts his death later.

- **Carbon isotopes** Another test identifies carbon isotopes, which are clues to what people have eaten over the years. The carbon in JR's bones shows that his diet consisted mainly of corn, the staple food of North America. If this individual had lived in England through adulthood, his bones would reflect a wheat-based diet. From the carbon isotopes, JR appears to have been born in Virginia. On the other hand, the tests for strontium and lead in his teeth show he was a European immigrant. These apparently conflicting results could be possible if JR arrived in the colony while young enough to take on the signs of his new corn-based diet.

- **Age** One of the most telling indications that JR was a young man is the incomplete fusion of the long bones in his lower legs. The top plate of JR's leg bone is not completely finished growing together, which indicates an age of 18 to 22.

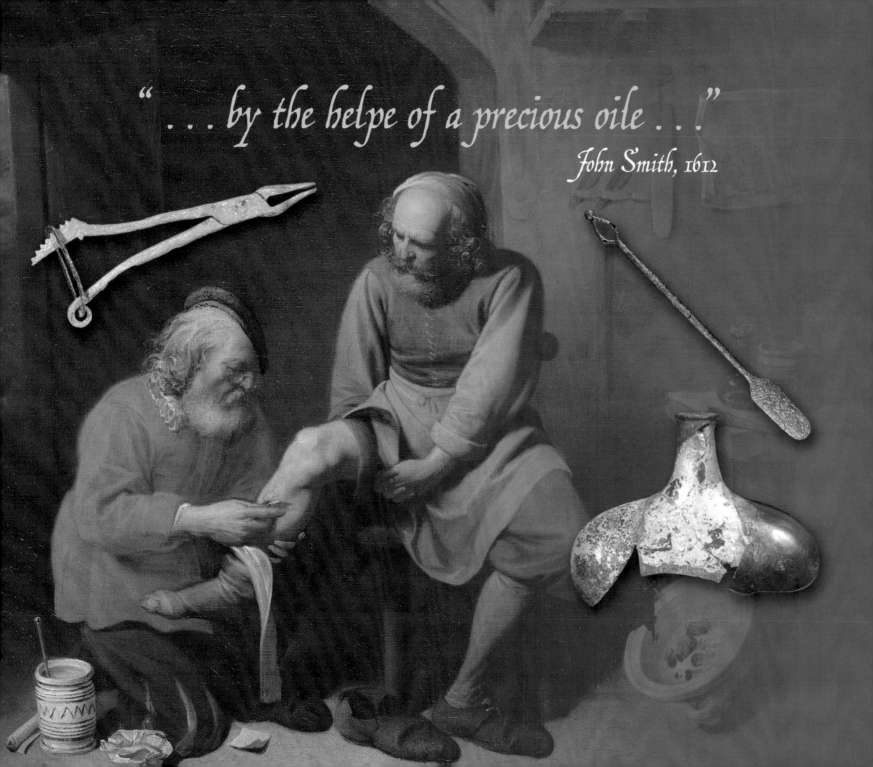

"... by the helpe of a precious oile ..."

John Smith, 1612

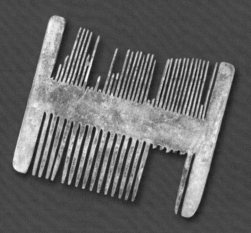

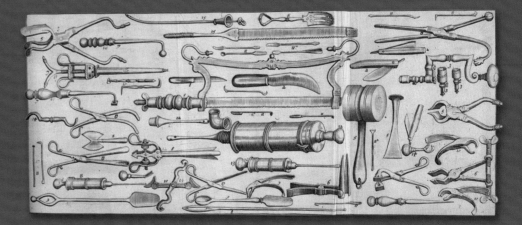

Health and Medicine

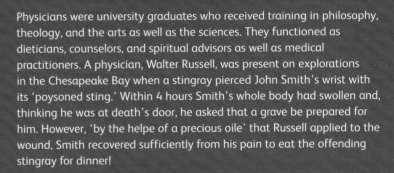

Physicians
Johannes Fleischer, May 1607
Walter Russell, January 1608

Apothecaries
Thomas Field, January 1608
John Harford, January 1608

Surgeons
William Wilkinson, May 1607
Thomas Wotton, May 1607
Post Ginnat, January 1608
Anthony Bagnall, before July 1608

Barber
Thomas Couper, May 1607

Men with medical training were essential for the new colony.
In the first year alone nine men arrived at Jamestown representing
the three major healing professions in the early 17th century.

Physicians were university graduates who received training in philosophy, theology, and the arts as well as the sciences. They functioned as dieticians, counselors, and spiritual advisors as well as medical practitioners. A physician, Walter Russell, was present on explorations in the Chesapeake Bay when a stingray pierced John Smith's wrist with its 'poysoned sting.' Within 4 hours Smith's whole body had swollen and, thinking he was at death's door, he asked that a grave be prepared for him. However, 'by the helpe of a precious oile' that Russell applied to the wound, Smith recovered sufficiently from his pain to eat the offending stingray for dinner!

Jamestown apothecaries, like modern day pharmacists, supplied the medicines prescribed by the colony's physicians. The dozens of colorful apothecary jars found at the Fort site, are clear signs that there was an ample supply of medicine at Jamestown, perhaps easing the pain of living in alien Virginia.

Surgeons were considered craftsmen and socially inferior to the university-trained physicians, because they cut into the human body. Aligned with the surgeons, barbers let blood and pulled teeth, as well as providing haircuts and shaves. Many surgeons honed their craft on the battlefield as they treated the wounds of war.

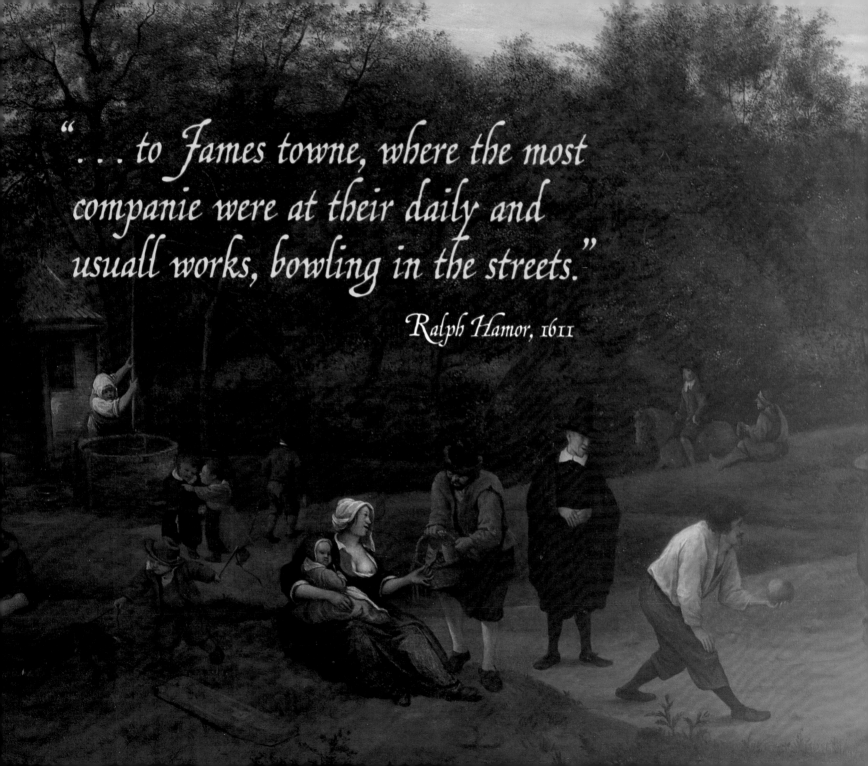

"… to James towne, where the most companie were at their daily and usuall works, bowling in the streets."

Ralph Hamor, 1611

Craft and Industry

The image of colonists engaged in idle entertainments instead of planting crops and providing shelter has come down to us as the cause of the lean and precarious times at Jamestown. Archaeology offers a fairer picture, one of energetic action taken by some of the colonists in their attempt to make the adventure a success.

Thousands of artifacts, including tools, equipment, and industrial byproducts, indicate many of the men actively worked toward their primary goal – to make money for the investors in England.

"These works to make return of present profit . . ."

The Ancient Planters, 1623

During the first year and a half, almost 300 individuals arrived at Jamestown for the purpose of turning a profit for the Virginia Company. The company instructed the men to establish a secured home base from which they could venture out to find, gather, and export any marketable resources the land offered.

Until he left Virginia in 1609, John Smith recorded the names of many of the individuals who arrived at Jamestown. Just over half are gentlemen, who guarded the fort and the Company's workforce. Others are described generally as laborers or tradesmen, but some are listed by their specific crafts. Archaeologists found many of the tools and equipment needed to practice trades. The artifacts, together with historical documents provide valuable insight into the individuals chosen to be among the first to develop Virginia's resources.

Cooper
John Lewes, January 2, 1608

Coopers produced the barrels to ship goods back to England. In a three-month period, for example, John Smith records the production of "3 or 4 last of pitch and tar," which amounts to about 50 barrels. Wooden barrels or casks also provided the best storage for the colony's provisions

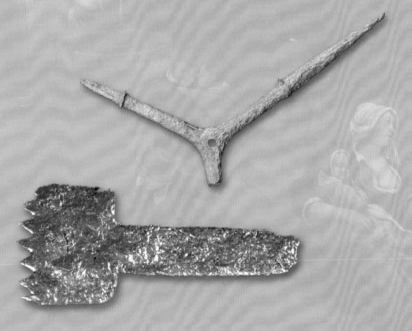

Blacksmith
James Read, May 13, 1607
Richard Dole, January 2, 1608
Peter Keffer, gunsmith, January 2, 1608

Some of the archaeological finds from the fort show that blacksmiths repaired both military and domestic iron objects, including recycling and modifying plate armor to make it more suitable for Virginia warfare.

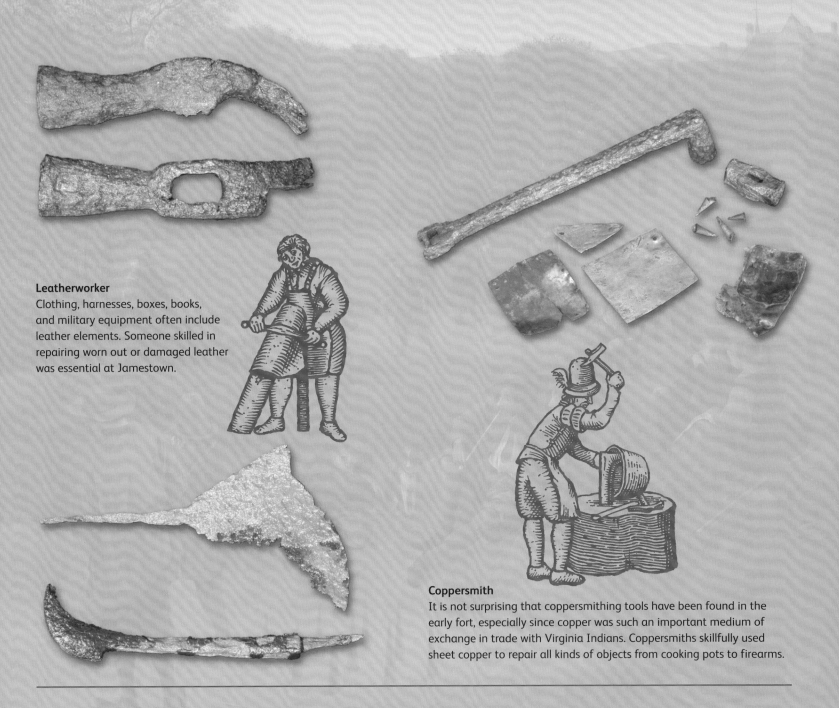

Leatherworker

Clothing, harnesses, boxes, books, and military equipment often include leather elements. Someone skilled in repairing worn out or damaged leather was essential at Jamestown.

Coppersmith

It is not surprising that coppersmithing tools have been found in the early fort, especially since copper was such an important medium of exchange in trade with Virginia Indians. Coppersmiths skillfully used sheet copper to repair all kinds of objects from cooking pots to firearms.

Tailors

William Love, May 13, 1607
William Ward, January 2, 1608
Thomas Hope, January 2, 1608
John Powell, January 2, 1608
William Young, January 2, 1608
William Beckwith, January 2, 1608
Lawrence Towtales, January 2, 1608

Clothing was in short supply in the early colony, but fort artifacts prove that the tailors were busy at their craft. It is likely they only served the gentlemen, as tailor-made clothing was expensive. Some of the tailors may have come as servants of the gentlemen, who were concerned that their wardrobes and those of the servants who attended them reflected their social standing.

Bricklayers

John Herd, May 13, 1607
William Garrett, May 13, 1607
Edward Short, May 13, 1607

The fact that bricklayers rather than brickmakers arrived in 1607 suggests that the very first colonists brought the few bricks they would need from England. With so much wood readily available for building, there was no need to spend time making bricks. Archaeological evidence indicates that bricks soon were made in the colony, but that they were confined to use for fireplace hearths. Not until 1638 was the first recorded brick building built on the island.

Glassmakers

Adam, September 29, 1608
Samuel, September 29, 1608
Francis, September 29, 1608

Three German glassmakers tried to establish a window glass factory at Jamestown. The windows were not for use in the colony but as a profitable venture to meet the window glass shortage in London. Archaeological evidence shows glassmakers labored two months in the fort to produce a "tryal of glasse" to send to the London investors. At some point, a glasshouse was constructed on Glasshouse Point, just off the island.

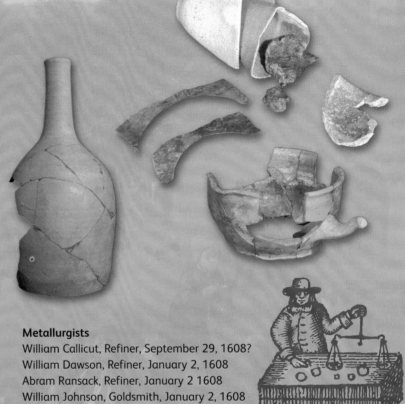

Metallurgists

William Callicut, Refiner, September 29, 1608?
William Dawson, Refiner, January 2, 1608
Abram Ransack, Refiner, January 2 1608
William Johnson, Goldsmith, January 2, 1608
Richard Belfield, Goldsmith, January 2, 1608

The colonists, convinced that they would find gold and silver in Virginia, began the search immediately after landing in May 1607. The first samples tested, however, "all turned to vapore." Goldsmiths were high status craftsmen and merchants who worked with precious metals. Refiners specialized in refining or separating precious metals.

In addition to searching for precious metals, Jamestown's metallurgists looked for other ores such as zinc. Zinc ores when heated with copper, form brass. During the 17th century, England depended on Europe for brass; it had abundant copper, but zinc was scarce.

Botanist
Johannes Fleischer, May 13, 1607

A 25-year-old German physician and botanist by the name of Johannes Fleischer arrived at Jamestown with the first colonists. He recorded the "exotic" Virginia plants and trees and searched for new medicines. Fleischer died at Jamestown in the summer of 1608 and his epitaph reads: "he surveyed what the German soil produced in terms of plants; what in America flourished, he viewed, too and thereby perished."

Carpenters
William Laxon, May 13, 1607
Edward Pising, May 13, 1607
Thomas Emery, May 13, 1607
Robert Small, May 13, 1607

Wood was the most obvious commodity the colony had to offer a timber-starved England. Tools found at the fort site show that the laborers and carpenters were hard at work not only constructing the fort and its buildings but also producing wainscot (finished trim) and clapboard (split planks) for export to England.

Jeweler
Daniel Stallings, January 2, 1608

English jewelers sold and appraised gemstones, but only rarely actually set the stones. Stallings probably searched Virginia for potential sources of gems. Semi-precious stones found during Jamestown excavations may reflect the collecting efforts of jewelers like Stallings.

Mason
Edward Brinton, May 13, 1607

Masons were stone merchants as well as the craftsmen who shaped stone and constructed masonry buildings. Brinton probably came to Jamestown to find stone that could be successfully marketed in London. Archaeologists have recovered many stone types that are not naturally found in the Jamestown area. Individuals interested in the value of such materials in England may have brought them to the fort.

Their

Corne new [...]

Their sitting at meate

The place of [...]

[...] wherm the Tombe of their Herounds standeth.

SECOTON

A [...] strange [...] about [...] lyke mens face

42

Copper for Corn

Farming had low priority for the London investors. In their eyes, hours spent laboring in the fields diverted focus from the principal goal -- generating commercial profit. The Virginia Company expected that most of the colony's food could be purchased from Virginia Indians using inexpensive pieces of copper and glass beads as money.

The Virginia Company sponsors worried that cultivation of large areas of land around the fort would send an alarming signal of permanency to the Virginia Indians. A peaceful relationship with "the naturals" was essential so the colonists could gain information about local resources and concentrate on crafts and industries without worrying about personal safety.

(the Virginia Indians) "attend a market which the English hold at their fort daily, and they bring the commodities of their land there to exchange for trinkets . . . "

Francis Magnel, 1610

The colonists engaged the Powhatan in active trade, realizing that the Virginia Indians were vital to the survival of Jamestown during its first years. In the beginning, the English traded inexpensive items they referred to as "trash" including small knives, mirrors, and straight pins. Glass beads and copper became the major currencies.

The English learned of copper's importance to coastal Indians in the 1580s, when they attempted to settle Roanoke Island in modern-day North Carolina. The Virginia Indians wore it prominently as symbols of status, even to their graves. In trade negotiations, even when they offered other trade goods, the colonists reported that "copper carieth ye price of all."

The Powhatan traditionally obtained copper from the Monacan to the west, but Indian warfare cut off that trade at the time the colonists founded Jamestown. Chief Powhatan saw Jamestown as his new major source of copper, perhaps saving the colonists, outnumbered by as much as 40 to 1, from serious attack.

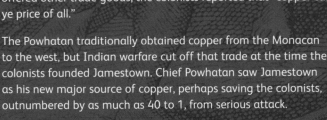

Money and Commerce

Their first charter granted the Virginia Company the right to mint money for the colony. It never did. There was really no great need for coinage at Jamestown. In the beginning, the company met most of the colonists' needs in exchange for the commodities shipped to England. Neither the investors nor the colonists felt this exchange was fair, until tobacco became the money of the colony.

Even a barter economy, however, needed a certain amount of currency. This is reflected in the over 400 coins, jettons, and tokens found at Jamestown. Transactions within the colony, like paying laborers or purchasing desperately needed supplies in black market dealings with sailors, required these monetary devices.

By the early 17th century, few people used Arabic numbers rather than Roman numerals when doing mathematical calculations. This, and a scarcity of pencil lead and paper, resulted in the widespread use of a visual form of accounting using casting counters or jettons.

Over 300 jettons have been recovered from the fort excavations. These brass coin-like objects were used much like an abacus. Calculations involved moving jettons over lines and spaces representing decimal units on a gridded counting board or cloth.

All of the Jamestown jettons were made in Nuremberg, most by Hans Krauwinckel and his nephew of the same name who worked between 1562 and 1635.

Since coins are among the few artifacts that are dated, they are welcome finds on archaeological sites. A coin found buried with other artifacts and undisturbed over the centuries sets the date after which the deposit occurred. But how much later? One 1560 coin found at the fort underscores the fact that coins could circulate for a long time during the colonial period.

Coins from England, Scotland, Ireland, France, Spain, Germany, the Netherlands, Sweden, Italy, and Livonia (present day Latvia) have been found at Jamestown. European coins were acceptable currency because they were worth the weight of the gold or silver used to make them. Some of the coins had been clipped to make "change," a necessary and common practice in England because of the chronic shortage of money in low denominations.

Two attempts used copper coins to meet the colonists' need for small change. The first is reflected in the over 30 Irish pennies and halfpennies found at Jamestown. Minted in London in 1601 and 1602, these coins provided Ireland with small coins while keeping silver in England. Rejected in Ireland, the coins must have been re-routed to Virginia. In 1613, England produced a coin with a face value of one farthing. Coated with tin to look like silver, the so-called Harrington farthing was not worth the copper used to produce it and was rejected in England. So far at Jamestown, 18 of these coins have been found.

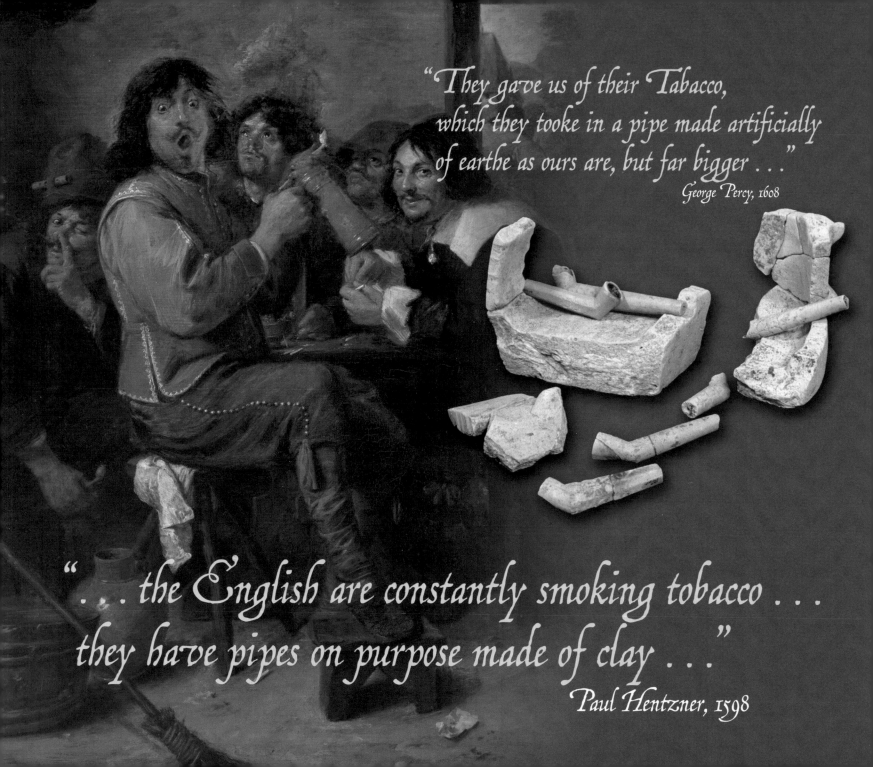

"They gave us of their Tabacco,
which they tooke in a pipe made artificially
of earthe as ours are, but far bigger . . ."
George Percy, 1608

" . . . the English are constantly smoking tobacco . . .
they have pipes on purpose made of clay . . ."
Paul Hentzner, 1598

The Golden Leaf

Archaeologists found hundreds of pipes for smoking tobacco, emphasizing the importance of tobacco in the lives of the colonists and the Virginia economy.

As early as 1573 the English adopted tobacco as a medicine, and treated their ailments by "the taking-in of the smoke of the Indian herbe called 'Tobac.'" The use of clay pipes for smoking appears to have begun soon after 1585, when English colonists saw American Indians using them on Roanoke Island. Some of these pipes, brought back to England, "caused many such pipes to be made."

Because tobacco was strong and expensive, the earliest English pipes typically have small bowls. According to one estimate an individual would have to smoke 25 early 17th-century pipes full of tobacco to finish just one ounce.

Early narratives describe the Virginia Indian use of tobacco in rituals. They made offerings of tobacco to calm storm-tossed waters or threw it into fire during religious ceremonies. Pipes filled with tobacco and shared by all present functioned as symbols of friendship, requiring much larger bowls than European pipes.

Colonists complained that Virginia tobacco, *Nicotiana rustica*, had a biting taste, not nearly as pleasant to smoke as the sweet-scented *Nicotiana tabacum* that grew in the West Indies. John Rolfe saw the potential for Virginia cultivation of the West Indian tobacco and, in 1612, began growing and curing the leaf experimentally for future transport to English markets. In 1614, he shipped four barrels of tobacco to England. Soon tobacco became the colony's money crop. The "golden leaf" had assured Jamestown's future.

> # "Thus we lived together,
> ## as if wee had beene one people . . ."
> ### John Smith, 1624

Meeting of Cultures

Documents indicate that Virginia Indian men lived in the fort and worked for colonists. Archaeological evidence suggests that native women were present as well.

One Virginia Indian man named Kempes lived at Jamestown for almost a year before he died of scurvy in 1610. While living among the colonists, he learned to speak English and attended church services. His new English "family" may have even given him a new name, for 'kemp' is an old English word meaning "brave strong warrior." Documents show another Virginia Indian hunted for one of the gentlemen in the fort and, according to John Smith, many others "had Salvages in like manner for their men."

Archaeological evidence of Virginia Indians in the fort includes a large number of Indian-made clay pipes and pots, and stone tools and traces of their production. These were in the first colonists' living areas and in their trash deposits.

"... nearest companion, wife, and bedfellow ..."

Ralph Hamor, 1615

The famous marriage of colonist John Rolfe and Powhatan's daughter Pocahontas in 1614 is thought to be the first between an Englishman and a Virginia Indian woman. But was it?

In 1612, Don Pedro de Zúñiga, the Spanish ambassador to London, informed his king that 40 or 50 Jamestown colonists had married Virginia Indians. Although this claim may be exaggerated, it must have alarmed the Spanish who saw such alliances as providing the English a firm foothold in Virginia.

But were the "marriages" reported by Spanish intelligence legally recognized unions or just informal and temporary liaisons? The same year Rolfe and Pocahontas married, none other than the governor of the colony, Sir Thomas Dale, declared that he wanted to marry Pocahontas' younger sister. It didn't seem to matter that he had a wife in England to whom he would return within two years. Dale sent beads, copper, hatchets, knives, wooden combs, fishhooks, and a grinding stone to Powhatan in an attempt to make the chief's daughter "his nearest companion, wife, and bedfellow." Powhatan refused.

A Moment in Time

Archaeology permits us to see small moments in time, to witness events in everyday lives not recorded by history. The remains of an early James Fort building, the Quarter, offers just such a snapshot of daily life. It is a moment frozen in time.

On the dirt floor of an early dwelling located along the east palisade wall, archaeologists found an interesting collection of artifacts. An earthen pot made by a Virginia Indian contained cooked turtle. Next to the pot lay a butchered turtle, the bones of a pig, and the charred remains of a fire. Nearby was a dagger still in its sheath, a leather bag of bullets, an Indian hammer stone, and a large glass trade bead.

These objects appear to have been abandoned suddenly, perhaps with the collapse of the earth and sapling roof. Whatever the catastrophic event, the occupants of the house never returned to reclaim their possessions.

Even though very crude, the structure, based upon the valuable objects found within, seems to have been a gentleman's home. The mixture of artifacts suggests the presence of a Virginia Indian at the Quarter, perhaps supporting a Spanish claim that, by 1612, a significant number of the colonists had "married" native women.

"... make yourselves all of one mind
for the good of your country ..."
Virginia Company of London, 1606

Religion

Jamestown was founded amidst the imperial conflict between Roman Catholic Spain and Protestant England. Individuals who refused to accept the English king as the supreme head over church and state were not officially welcomed in the new colony. Colonists suspected of being Catholic were considered spies for Spain.

In the first year, two colonists were publicly tried on religious grounds. The first president of the governing council in Virginia, Edward Maria Wingfield, suspected of being a Catholic sympathizer, was removed from office and sent to England. Fellow councilman Captain George Kendall, also suspected of being a Catholic, was executed at Jamestown.

Although these cases had religious overtones, they really stemmed from the social and political factionalism in the colony. Unlike Plymouth's pilgrims, Virginia's colonists did not leave England for religious reasons, but to extend England's territory and empire. So, even though the Virginia Company had resolved that the colony's established church was the Church of England, the unity and strength of the society were more important than any particular form of worship or theology. Emphasizing the worship of God and moral behavior over any particular religious view minimized conflict. Faith became a private matter at Jamestown.

Small Finds, Big Losses

The small portable objects archaeologists find offer insights into what people of the past valued. Prized as personal possessions, many of these artifacts were carried about in pockets, worn as jewelry, or used as embellishments to clothing. Some symbolized their owner's status and some revealed how the colonists spent their free time.

In 17th-century England, it was very important to display personal wealth through objects and clothing. With so many gentlemen coming to Jamestown in the first few years of the colony, it is not surprising that a number of artifacts reflect high status. These include expensive glassware, rare and valuable ceramics, gilded spurs, and silver threads. But even ordinary objects can imply high societal rank. A lead inkwell and brass book clasps reflect literacy, a skill of the privileged few who could afford an education.

Toys do not necessarily mean the presence of children. With none of the modern day amusements like television or computer games to occupy time, adults turned to games, musical instruments, and playthings they called "trifles" for amusement.

First Houses

House sites and household goods found in the fort give some indication of what the buildings were like, inside and out. Most of the men appear to have lived in crowded barracks-like conditions. Some of the gentlemen had the privacy of their own dwellings, even though a rudimentary pit house or tent.

Few could secure personal belongings in a locked room. Chests and coffers, as indicated by the numerous padlocks and hardware recovered in the fort, met the need for security. Some individuals may have been lucky enough to have a table and chairs, benches, or stools to sit on, but even simple chests, according to the records, could serve all those functions as well. Beds were the most expensive pieces of furniture at the time of Jamestown's founding. One iron bed bolt and many brass rings, used to hold curtains around beds, indicate that some had this luxury in the fort.

Very few candlesticks have been found during the excavations, attesting to the high cost of candles in the early 17th century. For most colonists, the only interior light after sunset came from fireplaces. Many of the colonists attempted to make the interiors of their dwellings more comfortable by lining them with what they described as "a delicate fine-wrought kind of mat" that they purchased "or snatched up" from Virginia Indians. Archaeologists found a fragment of one of these Indian-made reed mats located in an early pit house in the fort.

"*It were necessary that all your carpenters and other suchlike workmen about building do first build your storehouse and those other rooms of public and necessary use before any house be set up for any private person.*"

The Virginia Company of London, 1606

The Barracks

Following instructions, colonists first built company buildings, not individual houses. The remains of an early 17th-century building found in the fort, probably a barracks was likely one of these company structures.

Soil stains left by rotted structural timbers indicate that this barracks was long and narrow. It appears to have been divided into at least two rooms with a cellar at one end and a central wood and clay chimney. Like many of the other early buildings located in the fort, it was a Mud and Stud structure.

Mud and Stud was a building tradition common in the East Midlands region of England, particularly in Lincolnshire. A number of the early colonists were from that area and were familiar with this type of construction. Not working from architectural plans, the "carpenters and other suchlike workmen" erected structures using traditional methods.

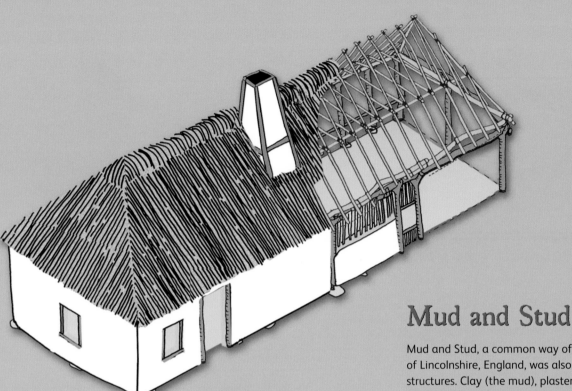

Mud and Stud

Mud and Stud, a common way of building in John Smith's home county of Lincolnshire, England, was also used to build some of the James Fort structures. Clay (the mud), plastered between and over vertical sapling slats (the studs), created a smooth exterior. A mixture of lime and animal fat waterproofed the exterior walls.

In this type of structure, saplings with forked ends served as studs supporting pole rafters. Crosspieces, placed between the studs, held vertical slats that supported the clay walls.

What did these buildings look like? Archaeological findings and documentary evidence suggest:

- The walls had a curving appearance as they followed the natural bends of the saplings.
- Small windows kept the interiors well insulated.
- Roofs were thatched with marsh grasses from Jamestown's swamps.
- Hearths had stick and mud smoke hoods.

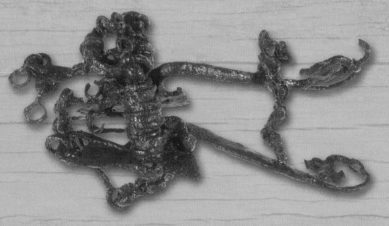

Desperate Times

"The Starving Time" lasted from the fall of 1609 through the spring of 1610. Two out of three of the colonists died from starvation, sickness, and Indian attack. Archaeologists have found evidence of this devastating period in the food remains of early pits.

Soon after the fall of 1609, when John Smith returned to England to seek medical treatment for a wound, Jamestown became isolated. Chief Powhatan applied pressure to the needy colony by forbidding his people to trade food and by ordering his warriors to attack any colonists they saw. Confined to close quarters within the fort and weakened by starvation, the colonists succumbed to sicknesses like dysentery and typhoid. Acting president George Percy remarked that during that time, "Indians killed as fast without [the fort] as Famine and Pestilence did within."

To survive, the colonists ate anything they could, including their shoe leather. The survivors speak of eating rats, cats, dogs, snakes "or what vermin or carrion soever we could light on." They even butchered the seven horses that had been brought from England the previous summer. These were desperate times at Jamestown.

Foodways

Many of the artifacts recovered at the fort relate to
the storage, preparation, and consumption of food
and beverages. These objects suggest what the colonists
ate and drank, where they got it, and even how they
prepared and consumed it.

> " *... fish in the Sea, foules in the ayre, and Beasts in the woods ...* "
>
> John Smith, 1624

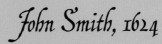

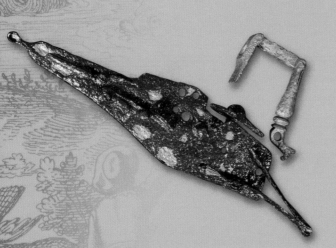

Hunting and Fishing

The colonists arrived with the equipment they needed to hunt and fish the bountiful forests and rivers of Virginia. Many were skilled at hunting and fishing for food, but in the new environment their weapons and customary hunting methods were more successful with some prey than with others.

Smith indicated that the colonists had great difficulty hunting and fishing. They probably found that the wilds of Virginia were nothing like the managed deer parks and stocked fishing ponds of England. Artifacts found on the fort site however, indicate that the colonists had the right equipment to live off their natural surroundings.

Excavated trash pits contained large quantities of fish bones representing 17 different species, suggesting that the colonists relied heavily on fish for survival. Sturgeon, a staple for the colonists, reportedly ranged in length from two to nine feet and could weigh several hundred pounds. From May to October, as they swam toward fresh water to spawn, sturgeon were plentiful in the James River by the fort. On one occasion, John Smith bragged that one throw of the net caught 68 sturgeon. In the spring following the Starving Time, the sturgeon failed to arrive during their usual season, perhaps deterred by saltier river water created by drought.

"for God would not have it so abandoned"
William Simmons, 1612

The *Sea Venture*

A fleet of eleven ships led by the *Sea Venture* left England for Virginia in June 1609. The *Sea Venture* never made it. Separated from the rest of the fleet by a Caribbean hurricane, the ship was blown toward Bermuda where it wrecked upon the reefs. Ten months later the *Sea Venture* survivors sailed into Jamestown on two new vessels they had constructed out of the wreckage and cedars growing on the island.

On board the *Sea Venture* were 150 passengers and crew including Sir Thomas Gates, the new governor; Sir George Somers, the Admiral of Virginia; John Rolfe, who was later to become known for his marriage to Pocahontas and for tobacco cultivation; and William Strachey, gentleman. It is through Strachey that we have the most compelling account of the *Sea Venture* wreck. Many scholars believe his *True Reportory of the Wreck and Redemption of Sir Thomas Gates, Knight* provided the inspiration for Shakespeare's play *The Tempest*.

The physical appearance of the Jamestown colonists, who were "so Leane that they looked lyke Anatomies Cryeing outt we are starved," horrified the survivors of the *Sea Venture* when they reached Jamestown in May 1610. The newly arrived group shared the food they stored for their voyage from Bermuda, which included live turtles and salted fish, birds, and hogs. Food remains from these Bermuda animals have been found in fort pits dating to 1610.

The unexpected arrival at Jamestown of the *Sea Venture* survivors during the Starving Time spring was the last straw. With food supplies running low and little hope for re-supply, Governor Gates decided to evacuate the colony. But as the colonists sailed down the James River they encountered a supply fleet carrying Lord De La Warr, the newly appointed governor for life. Veterans and newcomers joined to re-establish Jamestown.

With the arrival of De La Warr in June, and a year's worth of provisions for 400 people, attention turned from searching for food to rebuilding the deteriorating structures of James Fort. Laborers set to work "to cleanse the town" and archaeologists have found many cellars and trenches filled with trash from this renovation effort.

"We digged a faire Well of fresh water in the Fort . . . of excellent, sweet water which till then was wanting . . ."

John Smith, 1609

A Time Capsule

The colonists found no freshwater springs on Jamestown Island and, in the beginning, drank water from the tidal James River. Salt in the river water may have caused a variety of illnesses. There was no well on the island until late 1608 when John Smith reports digging "a faire Well of fresh water in the Fort of excellent sweet water which till then was wanting."

Over more than a century of digging, archaeologists have found 30 wells on Jamestown Island dating to the 17th century. Some are brick lined, but most are no more than dirt shafts with a wooden barrel at the bottom. The average depth is 12 feet.

Archaeologists found this brick-lined well just outside the 1607 fort. From studying the objects found both in the construction fill and inside the 14-foot-deep well shaft, they know that it was built about 10 years after the colonists arrived at Jamestown, and that it was no longer used by the mid-1620s.

Colonists collecting water lost a number of ceramic and metal vessels in the well, including a pewter flagon with the initials "PRE." Archaeologists believe this drinking vessel belonged to Richard and Elizabeth Pierce who probably fled to the island from their nearby home on Neck of Land following the 1622 attack by Virginia Indians.

The well became a useful place to discard trash after the wellhead collapsed and the water fouled. An entire suit of armor, agricultural tools, woodworking tools, and household objects were all found in the shaft. Some of the artifacts are still in useable condition. Why were they thrown away?

Well Ring

The brick-lined well was built upon a ring consisting of several sections of wood pinned together with iron spikes. The ring is the same diameter as the well and almost 3 inches thick. This provided a level surface upon which to place the bricks and enabled the well diggers to make the shaft deeper by undercutting the ring. The ring is made of red oak, a hard, heavy, and strong wood that is native to Virginia. Tests to determine when the oak was cut down, called dendrochronology, were inconclusive.

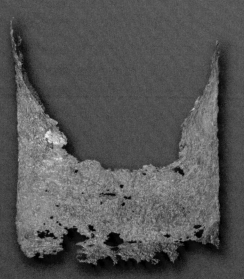

Digging a well

Artifacts in a well reveal the date when it was no longer being used for water, and was filled with debris. Objects found in the builder's trench that surrounds the shaft establish when a well was dug.

A careful reading of the soil reveals how workers built this well:

- First, they dug an over-sized hole to just above the ground water table. This trench created space for the workers to construct the final brick courses of the shaft, those from the ground water table up, from outside the well.

- They centered a red oak ring, the width of one brick and five feet in diameter, at the bottom of the hole.

- They laid several courses of brick upon the well ring.

- Then, workers undermined the ring by digging the dirt out from the inside, allowing the shaft section to sink slowly and evenly into the water-bearing soil.

- Once the well ring was deep enough to allow a steady flow of ground water, the builders bricked the shaft to the surface, filling the exterior working space around the open shaft as they went.

D. TENIERS. Fis

Conserve to Preserve

Archaeological conservation is the mechanical cleaning and chemical stabilization of artifacts; without it, some materials would completely disintegrate.

Iron objects, which are typically found covered in rust, are especially unstable. Before treating iron, conservators take non-destructive X-rays to determine how to proceed. Most often they use air abrasion, whereby fine powder under pressure breaks up the corrosion. Waterlogged artifacts, such as those recovered in wells, present a unique conservation situation. An anaerobic environment (one without oxygen) occurs below the water level. This slows the rusting of metals and allows organics such as wood, leather, and rope to survive. Conservators replace water in the organics with PEG, a polyethylene glycol solution that prevents shrinkage in the artifacts when used in conjunction with freeze-drying.

The cases in this exhibit have stable microenvironments to best preserve the conserved artifacts. In each case containing iron artifacts there is a desiccant known as silica get that helps to maintain a consistently low level of humidity. The conservators carefully monitor these levels and over time, many of the artifacts require re-treatment.

> " . . . som 16 or 18 houses, most as is the church built of brick, faire and large; and in them about a dozen families . . ."
> *The Rev. John Clayton, 1688*

The End of an Era

After James Fort was no longer needed and its palisades disappeared from the landscape, the site eventually fell into private ownership. Archaeologists found evidence of a late 17th-century structure in the fort area; one of the last to be built while Jamestown was still the colony's center of government.

In the second half of the 17th century, several people owned property in the old James Fort area including Colonel Nathaniel Bacon, cousin of the rebel by the same name. Archaeologists may have found the brick-lined cellar to one of two "very good" houses that Bacon built at Jamestown in 1683.

Artifacts in the cellar date it to the late 17th century. These include a dozen intact, but empty, glass wine bottles sitting on the dirt floor. One of the bottles has the personal seal of Francis Nicholson, Virginia's lieutenant governor from 1690 to 1692 and governor from 1698 to 1705.

Nicholson lived at Jamestown until the center of government moved to Williamsburg in 1699. Since there was no official governor's residence at the time, he may have resided in Bacon's house.

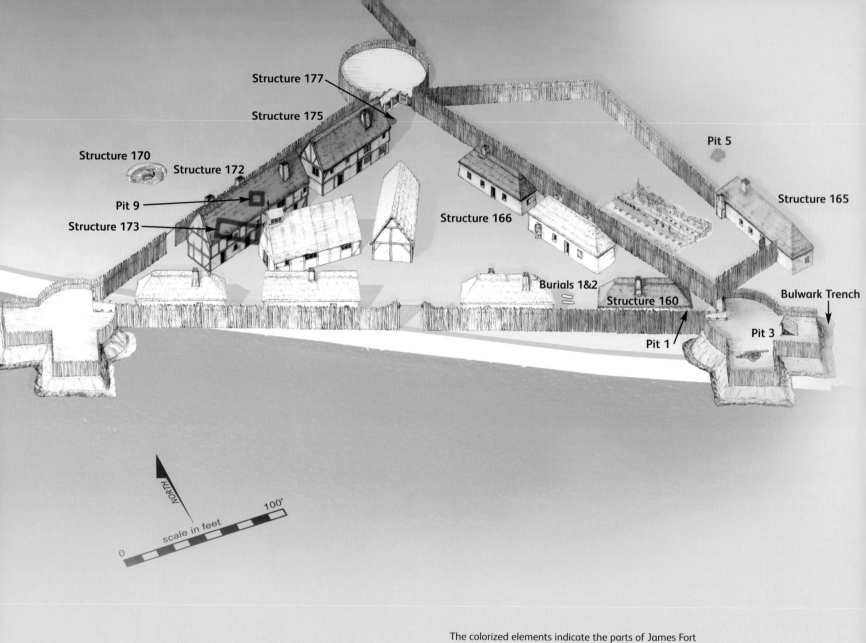

Structure 177

Structure 175

Structure 170

Structure 172

Pit 9

Structure 173

Structure 166

Pit 5

Structure 165

Burials 1&2

Structure 160

Bulwark Trench

Pit 1

Pit 3

NORTH

scale in feet

0   100'

The colorized elements indicate the parts of James Fort
that have been identified by archaeologists since 1994.
Graphic by Jamie May.

Contexts of Illustrated Artifacts

Bulwark Trench: Defensive ditch around bulwarks; early 17th century

Burial 1: Grave of JR102C; early 17th century

Burial 2: Grave of JR156C, ca. 1620

CF Burials: Burials within James Fort; ca. 1607-1611

Ditch 3: Ditch in southeastern area of fort; second quarter 17th century

Ditch 7: Ditch cutting through east bulwark; second quarter 17th century

Ditch 11: North south ditch located in southeastern part of the fort; mixed

Hunt Shrine: Soil disturbed in 1921 and 1960 by monument; mixed

LSG Burial: Graveyard beneath the 3rd and 4th Statehouse Complex; ca. 1610-40

Midden 1: Shoreline stabilization fill; second quarter 17th century

Pit 1: Trash pit at the end of Structure 160; ca. 1607-1610

Pit 3: Trash pit in the east bulwark; ca. 1607-1610

Pit 5: Soldier's pit house; ca. 1607-1610

Pit 6: Trash pit in north churchyard; ca. 2nd quarter 17th century

Pit 9: Soldier's pit house; ca. 1607-1610; covered by Governor's Row (Structure 172) by 1611.

Plowzone: Top layer of soil that has been disturbed by plowing; mixed

Project 100: 1955 National Park Service archaeological project searching for James Fort in the Confederate earthwork area; mixed

Structure 145: Confederate earthwork constructed in 1861 using re-deposited James Fort soil; mixed

Structure 160: The Barracks, a mud and stud building; ca. 1607-1610

Structure 165: The Factory, a mud and stud building with cellar and 3 brick hearths; ca. 1608-1610

Structure 166: The Quarter, a mud and stud building with cellar; early 17th century

Structure 170: Brick-lined well; ca. 1617-1625

Structure 173: Building with brick-lined cellar; post 1693

Structure 176: Brick addition to the eastern end of the Governor's Row (Structure 175); covers Structure 177; ca. 1617-1625

Structure 177: Wood-framed well beneath Structure 176; ca. 1611-1617

Transition: transitional layers between two known contexts; mixed

U. Trench 1: Telephone and electrical trench dug in 1938; mixed

Title page
Johannes Vingboons, *Caert* [chart] *Vande Riuer POWHATAN* [James River]
Geleg in Niew Nederlandt [Virginia], from *Atlas of the Dutch West India Company,*
c. 1638 (from c. 1617 ship's log) (detail)
Algemeen Rijksarchief, Den Hague, Netherlands

Page 3
left. Salt-glazed stoneware Bartmann jug with Italian coat of arms,
Frechen, Germany, early 17th century
Height 180 mm, Pit 1

right. Silver earpicker in the form of a dolphin, England or the Continent,
late 16th or early 17th century.
Multipurpose ear, tooth, and nail cleaner.
Length 50 mm, Plowzone

Page 10
Rendering of James Fort superimposed on the archaeological site.
The colorized elements indicate the parts of the fort that have been
identified by archaeologists since 1994. It is estimated that only about
40 % of the one-acre fort site has been uncovered as of 2007.
Graphic by Jamie May.

left. Tin-glazed earthenware dish, South Netherlands, early 17th century
Diameter 135 mm, Structure 145

Page 11
left. Lead-glazed earthenware saucer candlestick, Surrey-Hampshire border ware,
England, early 17th century
Height 62 mm, Structure 165

right. Cast brass mount in the form of a lion's face, early 17th century
Length 32 mm, Structure 165

Page 12

left. Marc Gheeraedts, *King James I* (detail)
Photo courtesy of The Colonial Williamsburg Foundation, Williamsburg, VA

top right. Cast brass mount in the form of a mermaid, early 17th century.
Length 42 mm, Structure 145

bottom right. Seal of the Virginia Company of London granted
by King James I in April 1606.

Page 13

left. Lead-glazed earthenware baluster fish jar, North Devon, England,
early 17th century.
Height 310 mm, Bulwark Trench

center. Lead-glazed earthenware butter pot, the English Midlands,
early 17th century.
Height 320 mm, Bulwark Trench and Pit 3

right. Unglazed earthenware olive jar, Seville, Spain, early 17th century.
Height 500 mm, Structure 165

Page 14

Johannes Vingboons, *Caert* [chart] *Vande Riuer POWHATAN* [James River]
Geleg in Niew Nederlandt [Virginia], from *Atlas of the Dutch West India Company*,
c. 1638 (from c. 1617 ship's log)
Algemeen Rijksarchief, Den Hague, Netherlands

Page 15

left. Silver English sixpence, dated 1607
Diameter 25.5 mm, Gift

right. Quartz crystal projectile point, Virginia, early 17th century
Length 29 mm, Pit 6.

Page 16

background. Map of Virginia 1608. Archivo General De Simancas (detail) (Ministerio de Cultura de Espana, M.P.y D IV-66)

left. Lead-glazed earthenware drinking jug, Surrey-Hampshire border ware, England, late 16th century – early 17th century
Height 190 mm, Bulwark Trench

right. Breastplate, iron, 16th century
Length 340 mm, Bulwark Trench

Page 17

left. Caltrops, iron, England, early 17th century
Used since Roman times to impede advancing cavalry and army.
Height 60 – 45 mm, Structures 145 and 173

top right. Linstock, iron, England, early 17th century
Held the matchcord used to fire the cannon.
Length 111 mm, Structure 165

center right. Axes and hatchet, iron, England, early 17th century
Felling axe: *Length 235 mm, Structure 165*
Broad axe: *Length 225 mm, Plowzone*
Hatchet: *Length 150 mm, Pit 3*

bottom right. Shot, iron, England, early 17th century
Shot for cannon known as falconets, falcons, sakers, minions, and demiculverins have been found in the fort.
Diameter: 1.7"- 4", Pit 1, Pit 3, Structure 165, Bulwark Trench, Pit 6, Ditch 3

Page 18
The Pikeman and the Musketeer from Jacob de Gheyn, *The Exercise of Arms*, 1607

Page 19
top left. Broadsword basket hilt, iron, Scotland,
late 16th century – early 17th century
Length 113 mm, Bulwark Trench

top center. Breastplate gusset, iron, England, late 16th century
Length 240 mm, Structure 165

top right. Dagger, iron with copper alloy hilt, England, early 17th century
Length 305 mm, Structure 176

bottom left. Powder flask nozzle, iron, England,
late 16th century – early 17th century
Length 133 mm, Structure 165

bottom, right. Cabasset helmet, iron, English, early 17th century.
Height 203 mm, Pit 1

Page 20
background. Jacob Willemsz, Delff II, *Officers of the White Banner*, Dutch
Gemeente Musea Delft, Collection Stedelijk Museum Het Prinsenhof, the Netherlands

left. Obverse and reverse Political jetton, tinned copper alloy,
Nuremberg, Germany, ca. 1580-90
Pierced to wear as a badge, this jetton warns of a false peace
between the Low Countries and Spain.
Diameter 28 mm, Transition

center. Horseman's axe, iron with silver damascening, England, early 17th century.
Length 170 mm, Structure 165

right. Gauntlet, iron, England, early 17th century
Length 115 mm, Structure 165

Page 21
left. Wingfield's Coat of Arms, Jamestown Church.
Three silver lures (bird wings and meat used by falconers to entice
their birds to return) on a red diagonal stripe.

center. Cast lead mount in the form of a lure, England, early 17th century
Possibly representing Edward Maria Wingfield, the colony's first president.
Length 52 mm, Structure 165

right. Buckler boss, iron, Wales or England, c. 1550-1575
Central element to a hand-held leather shield.
Height 140 mm, Diameter 125 mm, Bulwark Trench

Page 22
David Teniers II, *Country Kermis*, Dutch c. 1650
Rijksmuseum, Amsterdam

Page 23
Seal matrix, silver, England, early 17th century
Depicting the symbolism of mortality known as *memento mori*
and marked with the initials "LF."
Length 16.3 mm, Width 15.3 mm, Structure 145

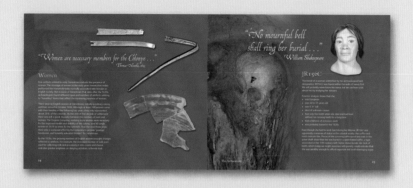

Page 24

background. Jacob Gerritsz Cuyp, *Young girl with a basket of eggs*, Dutch
Erich Lessing/Art Resource, NY
Louvre, Paris, France

top. Bodkin, copper alloy, inscribed "+E+S", England, early 17th century
Length 30 mm, Plowzone

center left. Bodkin, silver, inscribed "S.G.", England, early 17th century
Length 49 mm (inc.), OverStr165

center right. Bodkin, silver, engraved, early 17th century
Length 81 mm (bent), Plowzone

bottom. Lead-glazed earthenware milk pan, Essex, England, ca. 1630
Diameter (inc.), Midden 1

Page 25

Excavation photo of JR156C showing traces of the coffin wood.

Facial reconstruction of JR156C based upon her skull. This is the only known image of an English woman who settled at early Jamestown.
Modeling by Sharon Long.

Page 26

background. Excavation photo of the "usual burying place by James City" used in the years prior to the mid 1660s when the Statehouse was built over it.

Glass doublet buttons, copper alloy straight pins, and aglets,
c. 1st half 17th century
JR5087B was fully clothed when he was buried as indicated by the buttons that fastened his doublet and the aglets and pins that secured his breeches.
Button diameters 12 mm, LSG Burial

Page 27

top left. Ear Wires, copper alloy, c. 1st half 17th century
These wires were twisted up in JR5084D's hair, providing support for a hairstyle, when she was buried.
Diameter 45 mm, LSG Burial

center. Doublet buttons, copper alloy, c. 1st half 17th century
Located along the right arm of JR5057B, these buttons indicate this individual was wearing clothing when buried.
Diameter 11 mm, LSG Burial

bottom. Copper alloy aglet and English clay tobacco pipe, c. 1610-1630
The pipe was found with the remains of a pewter spoon in a dark organic stain indicating that JR5349B was buried with a pouch hanging from his belt.
Length of pipe 103 mm, Length of aglet 34 mm, LSG Burial

right. Excavation photo of Burial JR5349B.

Page 28

background. Photo of Otley Hall, Suffolk, England. This is the ancestral home of Bartholomew Gosnold and where he may have planned the Virginia venture.

left. Leading staff (detail), iron, English, early 17th century
Length 170 cm, CF Burials

center. Skull from burial JR1046B. Archaeologists believe this is Captain Bartholomew Gosnold.

right. Reconstructed face of JR1046B produced by computer modeling.

Page 29
Illustration of burial JR1046B showing location of the leading staff and the shape of the gable-lidded coffin.
Graphic by Jamie May.

Page 30
left. Facial reconstruction of JR102C.
Modeling by Sharon Long

center. Excavation photo of burial JR102C.

right. Xray of JR102C's right leg showing small pieces of lead imbedded with the bullet in the bone.

background. Photo of the controlled ballistics tests

Page 31
left. Lead musket ball and smaller pieces of shot from JR102C's right leg. The bullet was notched to create a dirty wound.
Diameter of bullet: 15 mm; Burial 1

Page 32
David Ryckaert III, *The Village Surgeon*, Flemish
Bildarchiv Preussuscher Kullturbesitz/Art Resource, NY
Gemaeldegalerie, Staatliche Museen zu Berlin, Berlin, Germany

left. Surgical forceps, iron, early 17th century
Length 178 mm; Structure 177

top right. Spatulum Mundani, iron, England, early 17th century
Surgical tool for the treatment of constipation.
Length 315 mm; Pit 3

bottom right. Pharmaceutical flask, glass, the Netherlands, early 17th century
Height 137 mm; Width 147 mm, Bulwark Trench

Page 33
top left. Comb, ivory, early 17th century
Length 41 mm, Pit 5

bottom left. Dental forceps, iron, England, with extracted human teeth,
early 17th century
Length of forceps 178 mm; Structure 177

right. John Woodall, 'A note of particular ingrediences for a surgeon's chest'
from Surgeon's Mate
University of Bristol Special Collections
London surgeon John Woodall sent a surgeon's chest to Jamestown in 1609.

Page 34/35
Jan Steen, *Farmers Playing at Skittles*, Dutch
Erich Lessing/Art Resource, NY
Kunsthistorisches Museum, Vienna, Austria

Page 36
Left
top. Triple auger, iron, England, early 17th century
Length of longest arm 150 mm; Plowzone

bottom. Croze iron, iron, England, early 17th century
Length 87 mm; Pit 1

Right
top left. Breastplate being cut up into iron plates for defensive garments known as jacks of plate.
Length 125 mm; Structure 165

top right. Jack Plates, iron, early 17th century
40 mm x 40mm; Bulwark Trench

center left. Rove strip, iron, early 17th century
Length 111 mm; Pit 3

center right. Hardy, iron, early 17th century
Length 93 mm : Project 100

bottom. Breastplate flange, iron, with silvered rivets, early 17th century
Length 215 mm; Structure 165

Page 37
Left
top. Upholsterer's hammer, iron, England, early 17th century
Length 95 mm; Pit 5

center. Shoe maker's knife, iron, England, early 17th century
Length 126 mm; Pit 5

bottom. Creasing iron, iron, England, early 17th century
Length 145 mm; Pit 5

Right
top. Hand swedge, iron, England, early 17th century
Length 235 mm, Pit 5

right. Planishing hammer head, iron, England, early 17th century
Length 46 mm, Pit 5

center. Sheet rivets, copper alloy, Virginia, early 17th century
Lengths 13 – 28 mm; Pit 3, Structure 165, and Plowzone

bottom row left and right. Tinker's dams, copper alloy, Virginia, early 17th century
Lengths 60 mm and 73 mm; Structure 165

bottom row center. Pendants, copper alloy, Virginia, early 17th century
Rectangular: length 65 mm, Structure 165; triangular: length 43 mm; U. Trench 1

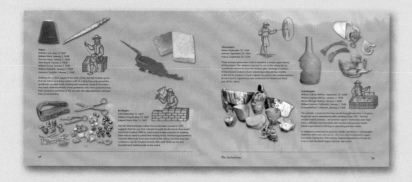

Page 38

top left. Thimble, brass, Nuremberg, early 17th century
Height 26 mm; Ditch 7

center left. Bodkin, bone, England, early 17th century
Length 73 mm, Structure 165

center right. Trowel, iron, England, early 17th century
Length 300 mm; Structure 176

right. Industrial bricks, clay, England or Continent, early 17th century
Widths 88mm and 120mm; Structure 165 and Pit 1

bottom. Assemblage of tailoring tools and dress accessories found in James Fort

Page 39

left. Evidence of glassmaking found within James Fort including melting pots
and Hessian crucibles, some containing glass and some containing glass gall
Pit 1, Pit 3, Structure 165, and Bulwark Trench

center. Distilling flask, earthenware, London, early 17th century
Height 375 mm; Structure 165

top right. Triangular Hessian crucibles with molten copper waste
Heights 8 mm and 9 mm; Pit 1

center right. Scrap, copper alloy, England, early 17th century
Lengths 97 mm and 115 mm; Pit 3

Crucible with copper residues on the interior, refractory clay, Germany,
early 17th century
Height 64 mm; Pit 3

bottom right. Dipper, earthenware, London, early 17th century
Height 53 mm; Structure 165

Page 40
left. Rasp, iron, England, early 17th century
Length 220 mm; Bulwark Trench

right. Tin-glazed earthenware apothecary jar, the Netherlands, early 17th century
Height 107 mm; Pit 1

Page 41
left. Virginia gemstones found in James Fort, including garnets, amethyst and quartz crystal, Virginia
Structure 165

right. Pick, iron, England
Length 23 mm; Plowzone

Page 42
John White, Secotan, c.1585 (detail)
© British Museum

left. Butchered Deer Bone, Virginia, early 17th century
Pit 3 and Bulwark Trench

top right. Freshwater Pearls, Virginia, early 17th century
Diameters 6 mm; Bulwark Trench

bottom right. Charred corn cobs, Virginia, early 17th century
Structure 177

Page 43
background. "Captain Gosnold trades with Indians,"
Americae pars Cecima, Openheim, v.6, 1619.
Courtesy of the Virginia Historical Society

Objects the colonists traded to the Indians in exchange for food included copper alloy dress accessories known as aglets, copper alloy bells, and glass and stone beads. Hundreds of these objects have been found in James Fort.

Page 44

background. Quentin Metsys, *The Money-lender (Banker) and His Wife*, Flemish 1514

Erich Lessing/Art Resource, NY

Louvre, Paris, France

Franco-Allegorical jetton by Hans Krauwinckel II, copper alloy, Nuremberg, Germany, c. 1589
Diameter 27 mm; Structure 165

Folding balance, copper alloy, early 17th century
Width 95 mm; Structure 145

Money box, iron, early 17th century
Height 76 mm; Structure 165

Page 45
Coins

1.   English sixpence, silver, dated 1602

2.   German sechsling, silver, dated 1629

3.   Irish penny, copper alloy, dated 1601

4.   Swedish öre, silver, dated 1576

5.   English sixpence, silver, dated 1582

6.   English penny, silver, 1619–1625

7.   English Harrington farthing, copper alloy, 1613–1614

8.   Spanish half real, silver, ca. 1580

9.   Livonian schilling, silver, dated 1577

10. English Harrington farthing, copper alloy, 1613–1614

11. Spanish four maravedis, billon, 1578–1598

12. English sixpence, silver, dated 1573

13. Dutch double stuiver, silver, dated 1615

14. Spanish maravedi, copper alloy, dated 1605

15. Spanish four maravedis, copper alloy, dated 1591

16. English halfpenny, silver, 1613–1615

17. Irish halfpenny, copper alloy, dated 1601

18. English penny, silver, 1591–1594

19. Scottish plack, billon, 1583

Page 46

Adriaen Brouwer, *The Smokers*, Flemish c. 1636

The Metropolitan Museum of Art, The Friedsam Collection, Bequest of Michael Friedsam, 1931 (32.100.21)
Photograph ©1989 The Metropolitan Museum of Art

Clay tobacco pipes and fragments of pipemaking saggars made by "tobacco-pipe-maker" Robert Cotton who arrived at Jamestown in January 1608.

Page 47

left. Tobacco from The Drake Manuscript.

The Pierpont Library, New York: MA39005.4V

top. Robert Cotton clay tobacco pipe, Virginia, early 17th century
Length 135 mm; Bulwark Trench

left. Virginia Indian clay tobacco pipe bowl, effigy of a bridled horse, early 17th century
Length 39 mm; Structure 165

center. Brick modified into a tobacco pipe bowl, early 17th century
Diameter 53 mm; Structure 165

right. Pewter tobacco pipe, early 17th century
Length 55 mm; Structure 145

Page 48

background. Theodore DeBry, *Hamor Meeting with Powhatan on Behalf of Dale*, 1614

Virginia Historical Society, Richmond, Virginia

left. Virginia Indian clay pot, shell-tempered and simple-stamped, early 17th century
Height 180mm; Pit 5

Right Virginia Indian clay tobacco pipe, early 17th century
Length 107 mm; Pit 9

Theodore DeBry, *Their Sitting at Meate*, 1590

Page 49

Mary Ellen Howe, *Pocahontas*, based on engraving by Simon de Passe

Page 50
Archaeological photo of Structure 166 with artifacts *in situ* on the pit floor

Page 51
top left. Virginia Indian clay pot, shell-tempered and scraped with mussel shell
Height 133 mm, Structure 166

bottom left. Charred wood remnants of cooking fire
Structure 166

right. Sheathed left-hand dagger, iron, early 17th century
Length 365 mm; Structure 166

Page 52
Bartholomeus van der Helst, *Portrait of an unknown Man
(probably a Protestant Minister)*, Dutch 1638
Museum Boijmans van Beuningen, Rotterdam

top left. Scallop shell ornament, enameled gold, early 17th century
Length 10 mm; Pit 5

top right. Scallop shell seal matrix, silver, early 17th century
Length 15 mm; Structure 145

bottom. Book clasps, copper alloy, early 17th century
*Length 118 mm, Pit 1; [bottom left]Length 42mm,
Pit 3 [bottom right] Length 43 mm, Pit 1*

Page 53
left. Crucifix, lead
Length 61 mm; Pit 3

top center. Crucifix, jet, early 17th century
Length 34 mm; Hunt Shrine

bottom left. Crucifix, copper alloy, early 17th century
Length 20 mm; Structure 177

right. Biblical jetton, copper alloy, Nuremberg, ca. 1585
This mathematical aid was pierced and threaded with a silver link
to wear as a religious medallion.
Diameter 28 mm; Structure 176

Page 54
Georges de la Tour, *The Dice Players*, French c. 1650
Erich Lessing/Art Resource, NY
Preston Hall Museum, Stockton on Tees, Great Britain

Page 55
Chess pieces, ivory, early 17th century
Length 35 mm, Pit 8; Length 23 mm, Structure 177

Gaming dice, bone and ivory, England and/or Continent, early 17th centuy
From 6x6 mm to 8x8 mm; Pits 1 and 3, Structure 165, Midden 1, Plowzone

Spur rowel, coppery alloy with gilding; early 17th century
Width 27 mm; Plowzone

Spur, cast brass with gold damascening, early 17th century
Length 82 mm; Plowzone

Chinese porcelain wine cup, Wan Li
Height 42 mm; Structure 165

Pocket sundial, ivory, Nuremberg, Germany, early 17th century
Length 57 mm; Structure 165

Trumpet mouthpiece, cast brass, early 17th century
Length 27 mm; Pit 1

Bagpipe mouthpiece, bone, early 17th century
Length 50 mm; Pit 3

Jew's harp, iron, early 17th century
Length 45 mm, Structure 165

Tambourine cymbal, copper alloy, early 17th century
Diameter 46 mm; Pit 1

Rumbler bell, cast brass, early 17th century
Diameter 25 mm; Pit 1

Page 56

Willem Cornelisz. Duyster, *Zwei Offiziere lassen sich Schmuck und kostbare Geräte zeigen*, Dutch
Kunstmuseum Basel
Kunstmuseum Basel, Martin Bühler

Page 57

top left. Padlock hasp, iron, England, early 17th century
Length 133 mm; Structure 165

top right. Staple, iron, England, early 17th century
Length 83 mm; Bulwark Trench

center left. Ball padlock, iron, England, early 17th century
Diameter 44 mm; Structure 165

center right. Padlock key, iron, England, early 17th century
Length 50 mm; Structure 145

bottom left. Chest hasp, iron, England, early 17th century
Length 107 mm; Pit 5

bottom right. Chest keyhole escutcheon plate, England, early 17th century
Length 72 mm; Pit 1

Page 58

Archaeological photo of Structure 160.

Interpretation of Structure 160 as a mud and stud building.
Graphic by Eric Deetz and Jamie May

Page 60

left. Curb bridle bit, iron, England, early 17th century
Length 215 mm; Pit 3

top right. Horse hoof coffin bone, early 17th century
Width 92 mm; Structure 165

center right. Dog jaw, bone, showing butchery marks, early 17th century
Length 128 mm; Pit 9

bottom right. Raptor beak and claws, bone, early 17th century
Structure 177

Page 61

left. Case bottle, glass, the Netherlands, early 17th century
Height 210 mm; Pit 5

top right. Box turtle carapaces, bone, Virginia, early 17th century
Modified for use by the colonists as drinking bowls.
Lengths 118 mm; Bulwark Trench

bottom right. Salt-glazed stoneware jug, Frechen, Germany, early 17th century
Height 220 mm; Structure 165

Page 62

Theodore de Bry "Sporting Life in the New World" from *America* 1618,
Virginia Historical Society, Richmond, Virginia

Page 63

top right. Sturgeon scute, bone, Virginia, early 17th century
Length 109 mm; Pit 1

left. Wheel-lock lockplate and cock, iron, early 17th century
Length 265 mm; Structure 165

center left. Double fish hook, brass, early 17th century
A specialized hook used in England for catching pike.
Length 33 mm; Structure 165

center right. Tubular net weight, lead, early 17th century
Length 65 mm; Ditch 11

right. Crossbow point known as forker, iron, early 17th century
Length 65 mm; Structure 165

Page 64

Thomas West, Third Baron de la Warr (1577-1618), Artist unknown, oil on panel, English, c. 1605.
Jamestown-Yorktown Foundation JY2002.02.
Gift of the Gladys and Frank Clark Foundation

Page 65

left. Cahow, bone, Bermuda, ca. 1610
A diving petrel with a 35" wingspan, these birds were plentiful on Bermuda when the English first arrived in 1609.
Length 60 mm; Pit 1

center. Signet ring, brass, England, bearing the displayed eagle family crest of colonist William Strachey; c. 1610
Height 22 mm, Ring size 8; Midden 1

right. Halberd blade, iron, England, c. 1610
Part of a ceremonial arm carried by the bodyguard of Governor Thomas West, the third Lord De La Warre. Griffin heads, the De La Warre family crest, decorate the blade.
Length 155 mm; Structure 165

Page 66

Detail of Archaearium exhibit interpreting the artifacts found at the bottom of the brick-lined well (Structure 170) including a Merida-type pitcher made in Portugal, a pig skull, iron hoes and axes, a boy's leather shoe, an iron pressing iron, an iron gridiron, and cast iron shot for a 6 ½ ft. long cannon known as a minion.

Page 67

Jan Brueghel (der Ältere), *Bauerngehöft mit Ziehbrunnen*, Dutch (detail)
Albertina, Wien

Pair of front and back gorgets, iron, England, early 17th century
Height 315 mm; Structure 170

Page 68
Excavation photo showing the red oak well ring from the bottom of the brick-lined well.
Structure 170

Page 69
Spade nosing, iron, England, early 17th century
Length 200 mm; Structure 165

Procedures used to dig Structure 170.
Illustration by Caroline Taylor

David Teniers the Younger, *The Village Holiday*, Flemish c. 1650 (detail)
Virginia Museum of Fine Arts, Richmond, The Adolph D. and Wilkins C. Williams Fund
Photo: Ron Jennings ©Virginia Museum of Fine Arts

Page 70
Artifacts from the brick-lined well, Structure 170, showing before and after some of the metal objects had been conserved. Close up of the conservation of an iron padlock using air abrasion.

Page 71
Archaeological photo of APVA Preservation Virginia staff archaeologist Jamie May excavating the brick-lined cellar of Structure 173.

top. Marked window lead, lead, England, dated 1693
Length 90 mm, Structure 173

center. Salt-glazed stoneware mug, Westerwald, Germany, ca. 1680
Height 87 mm, Structure 173

bottom. Wine bottle, glass, England, with the seal of Governor Francis Nicholson, ca. 1680-1700
Height 157 mm, Structure 173

Back cover
This is the only known 17th-century rendering of James Fort. It is illustrated on a 1608 map that is archived in Simancas, Spain.

Virtual Jamestown

Without the trained eye of an archaeologist, it is very difficult for the visiting public to visualize the features of James Fort from stains left in the soil. To compound the problem, few excavated features are left exposed to the destructive forces of nature for long. After mapping and photography, they are backfilled with a protective layer of soil and disappear from sight.

With the aid of the Virtual Viewers, Archaearium visitors are able to look out upon the archaeological site and see a reconstructed view of 17th-century James Fort. The Viewer provides flyovers of the fort and detailed information about specific areas as selected by the visitor. This technology is a very effective way of letting the visiting public "see" what the archaeologists "see."

The Flight Stuff

This small, 32 mm long, lead tag stamped "YAMES TOWNE" was recovered from the bottom of an early 17th-century well (Structure 177) in James Fort. It had probably been used to mark a container of goods that was shipped from England and, as such, it was the first object found by archaeologists marking Jamestown as an address.

In honor of the 400th Anniversary of Jamestown's founding, and in tribute to the spirit of exploration that continues with NASA's space program today, the tag was flown aboard the space Shuttle Atlantis to the International Space Station on June 8, 2007. One of the astronauts on the Atlantis flight, Mission Specialist Patrick Forrester, brought the tag back to Jamestown on September 6th after a trip that covered 5,809,363 miles.